"Jen Gluckow has mastered what it takes to "make it" in New York, and her book, Sales in a New York Minute, will teach you how to make sales anywhere. You'll learn strategies that when put into practice, will make sales faster and success greater. Every ultra high performer must read and must implement the strategies in this book."

-Jeb Blount
Best-Selling Author of 10 books including Sales EQ,
Fanatical Prospecting, and Objections

"Jen Gluckow is Smart. Savvy. Street wise. It takes one minute to read one idea in her book, Sales In a New York Minute. It will take you even less time to act on what you've read and the same amount of time to start making more money. Finally, a sales book that's actionable."

-Anthony Iannarino
Best-selling Author of The Only Sales Guide
You'll Ever Need and The Lost Art of Closing

"Some sales books offer practical, tactical steps. Some provide motivating reality checks. Sales in a New York Minute has all that and more. Every single page is pure gold."

-Deb Calvert
Author of DISCOVER Questions and
Stop Selling & Start Leading

"Whether you're new to sales or a seasoned pro, this book offers insights that will help you outshine the competition, stand out from the crowd, and close more sales. Jen Gluckow's Sales in a New York Minute is a must-have, must-read and must-implement book for anyone in the sales profession."

"P.S. It's fun, easy to read and engaging too!"

-Brynne Tillman
CEO at Social Sales Link
Author of The LinkedIn Sales Playbook

SALES IN A NEW YORK MINUTE™

JENNIFER GLUCKOW

212

212 PAGES OF REAL WORLD AND
EASY TO IMPLEMENT STRATEGIES TO MAKE MORE
SALES, BUILD LOYAL RELATIONSHIPS AND
MAKE MORE MONEY.

Sales in a New York Minute
© Copyright 2019 by Jennifer Gluckow.

Published by Sound Wisdom 717-530-2122.
info@soundwisdom.com

For more information on distribution call 717-530-2122 or info@soundwisdom.com.
For bulk sales discounts, call our friendly office 212-951-1153

The author may be contacted at jen@salesinanyminute.com
Website: www.salesinanyminute.com

Edited by Lisa Elmore & Alex Veng.
Cover and Book Design by Ashley Gadd.
Typesetting by Mike Wolff.

Printed in the United States by LSC Communications
First Printing, January 2019

Library of Congress Control Number: 2018954721
Gluckow, Jennifer
Sales In A New York Minute: 212 Pages Of Real World And Easy To Implement Strategies To Make More Sales, Build Loyal Relationships And Make More Money.
ISBN-10: 0-996207-72-4
ISBN-13: 978-0-9962077-2-0

NEW YORK:

IF YOU CAN MAKE SALES THERE,
YOU CAN MAKE SALES
ANYWHERE...
IT'S UP TO YOU!

JENNIFER GLUCKOW
@JENINANYMINUTE

FOREWORD

ONE MINUTE SALES COME-UPPANCE

BY JEFFREY GITOMER,
NEW YORK TIMES BEST-SELLING AUTHOR

I began selling in New York City in 1969. Making cold calls there –
and making sales. I found out immediately that I only had a minute to
establish both interest and credibility... A New York Minute.

When I met Jen Gluckow in 2014, I immediately knew she embodied
and embraced everything New York and New York City sales. And I
knew it in a minute.

Wit, grace, intelligence and balls – not just to "make it there..." – but
she also has the gift to convey it, teach it, and transfer her message.

212 is a symbol and a metaphor for this book.
It's the boiling point of water– and this book is HOT.
It's the NYC area code – and this book is NYC (and your city).
It's fast, bite-sized, info-bits and advice that you can immediately
implement and monetize.

Sales in any environment moves fast, and salespeople need answers fast
– faster than your competition. This book has 212 pages of fast answers
for your exact situation, that you can use the (New York) minute you

read them. And as if this book wasn't enough – go to Jennifer's special website (*salesinanyminutebook.com/workbook*), subscribe, and gain access to an implementation guide, your imple-mentor companion.

Over the past five years, I have watched her blossom on camera, on the platform and on the keyboard. Not just pretty, but pretty damn good. Not just smart, bold and moxie, but connected, networked and street smart. She speaks, writes, and shoots video with authority, charm and accuracy.

And this book is the manifestation of those qualities. Fast. Now. New.

Jennifer Gluckow isn't "the next big thing" – she's the "NOW big thing" and this book is her vehicle – make it yours, and you'll make more sales in your New York Minute.

Jeffrey Gitomer
*Author of The Little Red Book of Selling and
The Little Gold Book of Yes! Attitude*

HELLO, I'M JEN,
LET ME TELL YOU ALL ABOUT ME...

NOT.

You just bought (or you're considering) this book (thanks!), but you don't care about who I am yet.

You care about what value you're going to get from this book, what lessons you're going to learn, and what outcome you're going to obtain. I get it. And I'll get to the point - on the next page you'll find 212 reasons you need this book.

AND HERE'S THE NEW YORK MINUTE LESSON:

When you meet someone, don't talk about yourself first. Most people don't want to hear about the other guy until they have a reason to care. They want to talk about themselves. So ask them about their knowledge, their experience, their wisdom, how they got to where they are, ask them stuff you couldn't find out online, and that will get them to open up and tell you stories about themselves.

Once this book shows you how to win, make more sales, gain more profit, and create outstanding customer loyalty, then you may care more about who I am. When you do, you can flip to the back and find my bio.

Your customers and prospects care about how they win so when you make it about them, you'll be gaining more sales in a New York Minute. And you will easily do it, minute by minute.

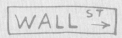

212 REASONS THIS BOOK IS FOR YOU

From attracting customers online and face-to-face, to helping secure lifelong relationships, earning referrals and reorders by building trust over time, to ensuring profitable sales and customer loyalty, you will learn strategies that when put into practice, will make sales faster and success greater.

212 IS A TRIPLE WINNING COMBINATION

1. **It's the boiling point of water.** And the boiling point of sales. Some people say if you add salt to water it will boil faster. I don't know if that's true, but I do know if you take my years of success that I boiled down to New York Minutes and apply them to your sales, your sales will heat up faster.

2. **It's the genuine, authentic, NYC area code.** It's the real deal and so is this book. My strategies, soon to be yours, come from making real sales - they are strategies that have worked for me and thousands of others who have implemented them. You can, too.

3. **It's the pages of mastery ideas and strategies in this book that will bring you success.** It's a reminder to pick up the phone and strengthen your ability to get through to the prospect. Your challenge: Make 212 prospecting outreaches a week. Whether you're a sales newbie or a sales master, this book will help you break through your competition, stand out from the crowd, and earn you more sales.

Bonus: You can read each strategy in under 212 seconds - in between meetings, while you're waiting for the decision-maker, or during your commute (don't read and drive - there's an audio version for that).

Bigger Bonus: Every New York Minute is easy to understand and implement.

THIS BOOK IS NOT ABOUT THE 5 STEPS TO
MAKING A SALE. NOR IS IT ABOUT MANIPULATIVE
OLD WORLD "CLOSE THE SALE" TACTICS.

EACH MINUTE IS ABOUT ADDING TO AND
REFINING YOUR SELLING AND CONNECTING
SKILLS. CREATING THE SUBTLE DIFFERENCE
BETWEEN YOU AND YOUR COMPETITION,
AND CREATING THE SUBTLE POWER
BETWEEN SALE AND NO SALE IN
A NEW YORK MINUTE.

Jen in a Ny Minute

HOW TO READ THIS BOOK AND MAKE MORE SALES IN A NEW YORK MINUTE

My job is to write each strategy and tell you how to implement it. Your job is to read each strategy, agree with it, believe you can do it, and then apply it. Then repeat the strategy until mastered.

As you read, mark the minutes that resonate with you, your sales, and your success.

After you finish the book, go back and study the action plans that can impact your productivity and success.

APPLY A MINUTE A DAY – LIKE A SALES VITAMIN. ONE A DAY. IT'S A LEGAL GROWTH HORMONE – SALES GROWTH.

If you love it, post it and share it on Twitter, Facebook, LinkedIn, Pinterest or Instagram! When you wake up in the morning, choose your New York Minute, decide what you are going to focus on implementing for the day and post your focus with #salesinanyminute and commit it to the (social media) world. Tag me *@jeninanyminute* and I will encourage you on your journey.

START HERE
IN A NY MINUTE

GIVE ME A MINUTE AND I'LL GIVE YOU A WORKBOOK.

GO TO SALESINANYMINUTEBOOK.COM/WORKBOOK
ENTER YOUR EMAIL ADDRESS

DOWNLOAD YOUR WORKBOOK

THIS IS NOT JUST A WORKBOOK. THIS IS YOUR
IMPLEMENTATION GUIDE. YOUR IMPLE-MENTOR.

"TAXI! ER, I MEAN UBER"

RAIN. Just when you need it most, there's not a cab to be had. Uber, that's New York City.

Everyone has heard the term, "in a New York Minute," and everyone has their own definition of what it means. Anything can happen in a New York Minute.

I think of a New York Minute as Fast. Clear. To the point.
And successful. Making it happen...no matter what.

People are on the go. Everything's fast - everybody walks fast, and talks fast. If you cold call them, they're gonna slam the phone down on you. If you knock on their door, they're gonna slam the door on you. Not because they're rude or not friendly, (well, yes they may be unfriendly), but because they're direct, they're busy, they're to the point. So, if you can make sales in New York, and figure out how to offer value, stand out and differentiate yourself from everyone else out there, you can make sales anywhere (or so the song goes).

ENTER UBER.

Uber disrupted the taxi industry forever. Fast.
Apple disrupted the computer industry forever. Fast.

As consumers, you and I seek answers online and our customers seek answers online, too. Our customers are WAY more knowledgeable than they've ever been, WAY more price informed than they've ever been and can Prime almost anything and have it at their doorstep in hours.

If you want to keep up with the fast and changing times, you need to make solid decisions, take solid risks, build solid relationships, offer value beyond expectation, stand out and differentiate yourself from everyone and everything else out there.

My concepts and strategies for selling in New York City follow Frank Sinatra's timeless line, "If you can make it there, you can make it anywhere." But it should be,

"IF YOU CAN MAKE THE SALE THERE, YOU CAN MAKE THE SALE ANYWHERE."

SALES IN A NY MINUTE

JENNIFER GLUCKOW

GET REAL! MAKE BANK!

MY PROMISE

I will bring real-world and easy-to-implement ideas and strategies that will help you become a better networker, create a better attitude for yourself, make more sales, and become a better person.

I will bring my NYC, straightforward, no BS, to-the-point attitude to you no matter where in the world you live.

I will be engaging, entertaining and full of energy.

I will offer strategies that will help you get past the gatekeeper, get to the decision-maker, overcome objections, demonstrate your value (in terms of the customer), close the sale, earn referrals and testimonials, and build relationships that create lifelong friendships.

YOUR PROMISE:

You will read and re-read these ideas and strategies. And you will implement them. When you're ready to take it further, have a peek at my YouTube videos, subscribe, share and leave a comment - I would love to interact with you and help you make more sales!

I WILL BRING REAL WORLD AND
EASY TO IMPLEMENT

IDEAS

AND STRATEGIES THAT WILL
HELP YOU BECOME A BETTER
NETWORKER, CREATE A BETTER
ATTITUDE FOR YOURSELF, MAKE
MORE SALES, AND BECOME A
BETTER PERSON.

TABLE OF CONTENTS

"HERE'S A SECRET: IF YOU WANT TO BE BEST.
IT DOESN'T HAPPEN IN A NEW YORK MINUTE.
IT TAKES 212 MINUTES."

JENNIFER GLUCKOW
@JENINANYMINUTE

#SALESINANYMINUTE

```
YOU
```

ALL ABOUT YOU AND YOUR NEW YORK MINUTE

It's all up to you...
All sales journeys begin with you!

How's your character? How are your characteristics?
How's your attitude? How's your belief?
How's your persistence? How's your creativity?
How's your commitment? How are your goals?
How's your work ethic? Who are you responsible to?
How are your leadership skills?

This chapter challenges your thinking about your character and your characteristics and will give you insight into how they'll make or break your sale in a New York Minute.

Discover your gaps in less than a New York Minute.

As you read this chapter, take an extra minute to rate yourself on these strategies and take action immediately to reinforce the concept. How well do you implement each one? Mark, dog-ear, fold down the page, highlight, or take a picture of the pages where you need to improve and you'll be on your way to improvement in a New York Minute.

SALES IN A NY MINUTE
JENNIFER GLUCKOW

HOW'S YOUR ATTITUDE?
ATTITUDE: THE FIRST MINUTE!

Attitude, your attitude, affects everything you do and every accomplishment you achieve, or don't achieve.

Pretty important... *but*, some people don't think attitude is that important. Those people are wrong.

GRAB YOUR IMPLE-MENTOR:

- **Think about the five most successful people you know.** How's their attitude?
- **Think about Olympic athletes, entrepreneurs.** How does their attitude, their "self-talk" affect their success and their outcomes?
- **Now think about salespeople.** When a successful salesperson loses a sale, they don't bring that bummed-out attitude into the next sale.
- **Now think about you.** In life, there are negative aspects that can get in the way of your attitude...but only if you let them. Ever call a close friend or family member on the phone and they answer,

"Hello" in a very sad, deep tone? Obviously, they are trying to tell you something without actually saying much of anything – that everything is not okay. Answer happy. Talk happy.

- **Now think about how you respond.** From an attitude perspective, what's the best way to respond to their tone? The answer is, to ask a question that doesn't include the word, "why." Asking why makes people defensive, and it tends to breed an answer that's not the whole answer. Think about the times that you have been asked why and why you don't give a full answer. Especially if it's a parent, sibling, or a very close friend.

While you can't control other people's unhappiness, you *can* control yours and you can *choose* your attitude in a New York Minute.

THINK ABOUT THE FIVE MOST SUCCESSFUL PEOPLE YOU KNOW.

HOW'S THEIR ATTITUDE?

"

APPROACH EVERYTHING YOU
DO WITH A POSITIVE MINDSET.

SHOWER HAPPY.

BRUSH YOUR TEETH HAPPY.

PEE HAPPY.

BE HAPPY.

JENNIFER GLUCKOW
@JENINANYMINUTE

ATTITUDE ANTIOXIDANT

Achoo! It's attitude flu season, here's what you can do to build your attitude fortitude and attitude antioxidant immunity...

YOUR ACTION:

- **Make a morning routine that sets the tone for your day.** Smile in your mirror, read positive, write positive, watch positive.
- **Clear your mind of the clutter from your to-dos.** Write them down, so you don't forget, and don't have to remember them.
- **Start happy.** Approach everything you do with a positive mindset. Shower happy. Brush your teeth happy. Pee happy. Be happy.
- **Look good.** If you look good, you'll feel good, and think good.
- **Check in with yourself.** Someone pissing you off? Why? How are you reacting? Set your actions and reactions to positive.
- **Help yourself.** If you find yourself unhappy, ask yourself why. *Note:* asking yourself why is different than asking others. Be honest with yourself. Write about it to yourself.
- **Use attitude antioxidants.** Take a bath, shower or steam shower, listen to music, meditate, watch comedy, go for a walk, work out. C'mon, sweat a little, OK, ice cream works too!

Whatever you choose, have fun and think fun and you'll be improving your attitude in a New York Minute.

SALES IN A NY MINUTE
JENNIFER GLUCKOW

IT'S A ~~BEAUTIFUL~~ BAD DAY IN THE NEIGHBORHOOD! (YOUR CHOICE)

Ever hear someone say they're having a challenging day - a bad day - all day?

I'm *sure* you've never said that.
But if you have, ask yourself, whose fault is that?
Bad days are usually self-inflicted.

Here's how to go from bad to good:

- Change something to snap out of it. Break the bad day.
- Pause. Take a reality check and look for the good.
- Quit the excuses - stop blaming it on the day, "Oh, today's just one of those days." What's blaming it on the day gonna solve? Put your big boy pants on (or big girl pants) and go have a good day!
- And if Mondays are always bad days, then you need to find a new job, one you love.

When things keep going a different way - and that way is not your way - your job is to figure out what you can do to make it a *great* day.

Every day is exactly the same, except for:
1. How you choose to treat it.
2. The opportunities you choose or fail to take advantage of.
3. The people you choose to talk to and interact with.
4. The activities you choose to do or not do.

You have the personal power (and responsibility to yourself) to take control of the bad and shake it out.

GRAB YOUR IMPLE-MENTOR:

The next time it feels like the world is crumbling, make a list of 5 things you're grateful for. Can't think of 5? List 3. That will help your mood.

AND HERE'S THE KEY:

The best thing to do is prevent a bad day. Start your day off with a kick-ass morning routine (like *The Miracle Morning*) and you'll be on your way to better days in a New York Minute.

"IF MONDAYS ARE
ALWAYS BAD DAYS,
THEN FIND A NEW JOB,
ONE THAT WILL HELP YOU
LOVE MONDAYS"

JENNIFER GLUCKOW
@JENINANYMINUTE

NEGATIVITY BLOCKS CREATIVITY

If you've ever been in an argument with someone, walked away, and after a minute or two thought to yourself, "Ah, I should have thought of this or, I should have said that...," it's because your negativity was blocking your creativity in the moment. The minute you became peaceful again, you had a creative thought.

MAKE IT HAPPEN:

THE MORE YOU CAN
STAY PEACEFUL, AND IN
(SELF) CONTROL, THE
MORE GREAT IDEAS
YOU'RE GONNA HAVE
IN A CREATIVE
NEW YORK MINUTE.

SELLING IN THE RAIN...

Sing it!
Don't let the rain affect your selling attitude.

When it's raining in NYC, it's hard to get a cab (or Uber).
It's more crowded. Umbrellas everywhere. The streets are full of
splashing cars and people wanting to avoid getting wet.

And rain can affect your attitude when you walk into a sale. Especially
if you're walking in after you just got rejected from the last sale.

Here's the sunshine clue: If you love selling and you love your job,
ignore the weather.

Hot, cold, rain, sleet, snow, you're the mailman (or mailwoman) of
sales and nothing can deter you from getting out there and helping
customers buy from you.

DO THIS:

Walk into that sale, dripping wet, and with a great attitude, say,
"I love this kind of weather! Because most of my competitors stay
home." Don't be a fair-weather salesman. Sell in the rain. And you'll
create your own rainbow in a New York Minute.

"

HOT, COLD, RAIN, SLEET, SNOW,

YOU'RE THE MAILMAN (OR MAILWOMAN) OF SALES

AND NOTHING CAN DETER YOU FROM GETTING OUT THERE

AND HELPING CUSTOMERS BUY FROM YOU.

JENNIFER GLUCKOW
@JENINANYMINUTE

9

"YOUR ACTIONS ARE NOT JUST INTENTIONS,
THEY'RE YOUR CHOICES. AND YOU, AND ONLY YOU,
MAKE THOSE CHOICES IN A NEW YORK MINUTE."

JENNIFER GLUCKOW
@JENINANYMINUTE

SALES IN A NY MINUTE
JENNIFER GLUCKOW

WHICH SUBCONSCIOUS ACTIONS LEAD TO SALES?

Goals are intentions to achieve. When you wake up in the morning subconsciously, you have already made a decision about what you are going to do that day. Those are your intentions. If you can combine your intentions with the goals that you have set, then the actions that you take will lead you to achievement. Your actions are not just intentions, they're your choices. And you, and only you, make those choices in a New York Minute.

GRAB YOUR IMPLE-MENTOR:

Before you go to sleep, make a list of what you are going to do when you wake up. If you're trying to stay in shape or lose weight, this could include working out or making a healthy breakfast. Also write down 3-5 accomplishments you intend to achieve (they can be work or personal). This way, you'll have a plan when you wake up. Then it's up to you to make the right choices to accomplish your plan throughout the day.

> **SOME PEOPLE SAY THAT FIRST IMPRESSIONS ARE MADE WITHIN**
>
> # 7 SECONDS.
>
> I SAY FIRST IMPRESSIONS ARE MADE
>
> ## WAAAY BEFORE THAT

JENNIFER GLUCKOW
@JENINANYMINUTE

WHAT ARE YOUR INTENTIONS?

Intention is not about a single activity or building a single relationship. It's about making a five-year plan, so that when you make cold calls, go to networking events, build customer relationships, and invest in your salesman(lady)ship, it's with the intention to get to know people, be known by people as a person of value, give value to others without expectation, and whenever possible, be the leader.

DO THIS:

Intention insight: To begin with intention, think about the outcome you are hoping for. What do you want to get by your actions, efforts, and outputs? What are your specific goals? Whatever it is, set your intention to become the best and surround yourself with the best.

Your "what" intention: Determines actions and potential outcomes.

Your "where" intention: Determines the best place and best groups to help you achieve those outcomes.

Your "when" intention: Determines when you can achieve your outcomes/goals or how much time you need to invest to achieve your desired outcomes.

Determine your intentions and create your five-year plan. Invest time in your intended achievement each day and you'll be dominating your intentions and achieving positive outcomes in a New York Minute.

SALES IN A NY MINUTE
JENNIFER GLUCKOW

WHAT'S YOUR THIRD "WHY"?

To increase your sales and success, you need to identify your DEEPEST "why," you know, the reason behind your work. The reason you do what you do! You may have thought about it, but never identified your "why" before. Or if you're like most people, you may have never given it an ounce of thought. Whether you are new to sales or have been selling for the past 20 years, **"why"** applies to you.

Once you identify your REAL why, AKA your true driving success purpose, you will be on a mission-driven path. The power of purpose creates laser-beam energy and focus, and it's that energy and focus that will help you win.

Once you know your why, nothing will stop you - you'll take risks, overcome obstacles, and figure out how in a New York Minute.

GRAB YOUR IMPLE-MENTOR:

Think about your why and write it in your workbook. Then keep pressing yourself until you come up with your third or fourth "why" - your real why. Go write it down!

Here's the process: If you wrote down that your why is to make a lot of money, ask yourself, "Why?" Why do you want to make a lot of money? And keep asking yourself why until you get the real reason, the reason that contains your emotion. You may have to ask "why?" multiple times and keep digging until you get the real answer.

Once you get to the heart of your emotion, let that drive everything you do. Put a daily reminder of it on your phone home screen, your computer, or your office wall - look at it often.

SALES IN A NY MINUTE
JENNIFER GLUCKOW

YOUR THOUGHTS DETERMINE YOUR ACTIONS, AND YOUR ACTIONS DETERMINE YOUR OUTCOME

Your thoughts will determine your outcome. If you make excuses, you'll rely on excuses. If you take responsibility, you'll rely on yourself and, you'll get the achievements you're hoping for.

PERSONAL EXAMPLE

I was on my Peloton bike and tracking behind my usual output level. It was 15 minutes into the class and I started making excuses for myself - I woke up late, I was tired, my legs were sore from yesterday's workout. I could have kept going with excuses, but then it hit me...my thoughts were controlling my outcome. And my outcome was subpar because my thoughts were subpar. You ever do that?

I started saying to myself, "I can beat my personal record. I'm gonna beat my personal record." As I said that in my head, my feet started pedaling faster. I turned up the resistance. My output was stronger - there was a noticeable difference. And then, the instructor said, "Lift the corners of your mouth." SMILE! I found myself smiling, having fun, and pedaling faster and harder than before. I started catching up to my personal record and then I beat my personal record.

Imagine, if I kept allowing myself excuses? I would have finished the class with a less than excellent output, and I would have thought it was okay because I had justified it. *Ever allow yourself excuses? Change that to NEVER allow yourself excuses!*

SALES SITUATION:

You're meeting with a prospect and you feel like the meeting isn't going that well and you start telling yourself it's okay. You blame the customer - the customer doesn't have any budget right now, or they're gonna stick with their vendor because they're embedded with them, or they have a relationship with them, or they just don't get it. You start giving yourself every excuse possible why you're gonna lose the sale. And you start blaming the customer for why you're about to lose. Those thoughts are pedaling you down Loser Avenue. Believe me on this one: If you believe you will lose, and you make excuses for why you will lose, you will lose! Your thoughts are that powerful.

Believe you will win before you enter the meeting. Tell yourself you're going to leave with a new customer - that you're going to win the deal. Believe that you can and you most likely will in a New York Minute.

GRAB YOUR IMPLE-MENTOR:

Every time you hear yourself making an excuse, write it down and turn it into a responsibility-taking statement.

THINKING ABOUT THINKING

"We become what we think about most of the time, and that's the strangest secret," said the late, great Earl Nightingale.

What are you thinking about most of the time?

How often are you thinking strategically about your business, your sales, your clients, your future? I'm sure you would agree that thinking is important, but how often do you schedule time with yourself to think? Time that's uninterrupted, time without text or app notifications, time without checking Snapchat or Facebook or Instagram, time in silence and solitude to think?

HERE'S HOW TO MAXIMIZE AND MASTER YOUR THINKING EFFECTIVENESS:

- **Schedule time on your calendar.** Aim for the same time every day and make it a routine. Make this time with yourself sacred - let nothing get in the way.
- **Clear your head before you begin.** I have been using a meditation app called Headspace, and find that my ideas are exploding after I slow down and rest my mind.
- **Drain your brain before you begin.** Let go of any negativity. It's hard to be creative with negative thoughts in the background.

- **Be totally alone. Remove distractions.** Silence your phone and put it face down. Forget the alerts. Almost anything can wait 20 minutes. No Google, no texting, no angry birds, seriously if you're concentrating on shooting the bird... "You become what you think about." Think about that one.
- **Music or background noise.** If it helps you zone out, classical on low volume is best. Music without words.
- **Create a peaceful thinking place.** It should be open and inspiring. Aim for greenery and natural sunlight.
- **15 minutes a day.** You don't become thoughtful and self-empowering in a day. It takes days, months and years. But it starts with a day. Invest 15 minutes a day (minimum!) thinking for yourself. As it gets easier and you see it become fruitful, increase this time each day.
- **Write them down.** The minute you get a thought or idea, write it down. Create a thought file and flesh out your ideas. The key is to save your thoughts and document your ideas.

Now that I've got you thinking about thinking, what's your plan?

- When are you going to think? Where are you going to think?
- Got it scheduled?
- What are you going to do with your thoughts?
- What kind of action will you take?

GRAB YOUR IMPLE-MENTOR:

Answer these questions with your actionable intentions and you'll be on a better thinking path that will last a lifetime in a New York Minute.

THINKING ABOUT THINKING?

SET YOUR ALARM CLOCK TO DEDICATED, FOCUSED THINK TIME.

JENNIFER GLUCKOW
@JENINANYMINUTE

SALES IN A NY MINUTE
JENNIFER GLUCKOW

CHANGE YOUR "THOUGHT LANGUAGE" AND YOU'LL CHANGE YOUR OUTCOMES

Never say the words, "I'm struggling with," it's a sign of weakness and your inability or fear to take affirmative action. Instead say, "Here's what I'm thinking…" When you do this, it forces you to "think it out" rather than "struggle with it."

Just a "thought" that can change your outcome in a New York Minute.

GO TO:

procabulary.org and sign up for their Core Language Upgrade course. They will help you learn "the language of getting things done."

SALES IN A NY MINUTE
JENNIFER GLUCKOW

GET ME TO THE
BARRE ON TIME

I got to Barre class at 5:44 a.m. thinking I was a minute early but, I was 14 minutes late! They don't let you in when you're 14 minutes late, so I had to drive back home pissed off. Pissed off because I couldn't work out. Pissed off because I woke up early for class, and I was blaming them.

After a few seconds of blaming, I realized it's not their fault. I needed to take responsibility that I showed up at the wrong time. I didn't check the schedule.

What do you do when something goes wrong or doesn't go your way? Do you blame or do you take responsibility? How do you get yourself back into that mindset, so that you can make the sale no matter what?

HERE'S YOUR SALES CHALLENGE:

First you need to sell yourself mentally to accept responsibility. Your mindset determines everything. Go out and make the sale. Make the sale to yourself and you'll be making more sales to your clients in a New York Minute.

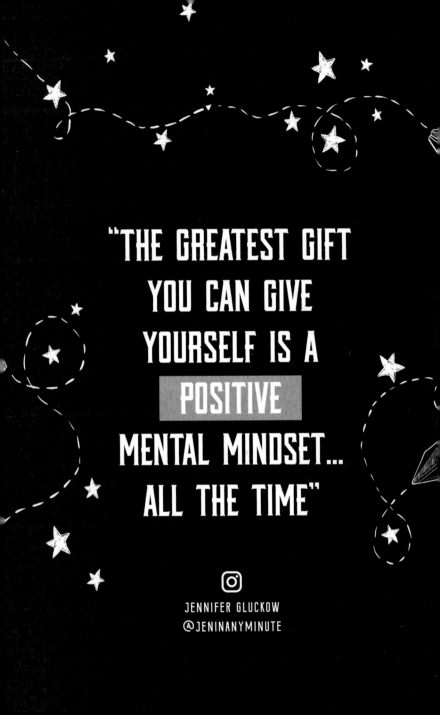

"THE GREATEST GIFT
YOU CAN GIVE
YOURSELF IS A
POSITIVE
MENTAL MINDSET...
ALL THE TIME"

JENNIFER GLUCKOW
@JENINANYMINUTE

BLAME VS. RESPONSIBILITY

PERSONAL STORY:

It was a freezing cold, snowy day, and I was off to make the sale! Except the building I was looking for didn't exist. Building #32, the building where I was supposed to meet with a group of people, present/educate, and make the sale, was missing.

I asked nearby retailers about #32, but no one knew where it was. I emailed, called, and texted people in the meeting, but no one responded.

There I was in the middle of Manhattan, in high heels, carrying a heavy bag, with my big projector, my computer, all my winter clothing, and I'm schlepping all this stuff and can't find the meeting location. My 45-minute early arrival was turning into a late arrival.

And then I found out that the prospect had given me the wrong address. You can imagine, I was pissed off. Very pissed off (and sweaty in 10°F weather).

As I approached the right building, I realized, they don't care about what happened to me. They've been upstairs talking, not checking their phones, having a good time. And they don't care that I've been looking for #32 for almost an hour, or that I'm stressed out and upset. They just want me to show up prepared, with a great attitude and ready to perform.

Two Options: Go upstairs and blame my contact - show them on my email that I was given the wrong address, or take responsibility and make the sale.

Pause: You know what I needed to do and I had less than a New York Minute to change my mood.

New York Minute Moral: Take responsibility and you'll be making more sales in a New York Minute (I did, and I did!).

YOUR ACTION:

Go back and re-read my New York Minute attitude strategies (see the attitude section) and choose your best attitude every day.

YOUR MINDSET
DETERMINES
EVERYTHING.

DO YOU BELIEVE? SIX BELIEFS TO UNLOCK SALES SUCCESS

If you are a top salesperson or you're trying to become one, you need the following six beliefs:

- Belief in yourself, that you are the best
- Belief in your abilities to help others win
- Belief that your company is the best
- Belief that your product or service is the best
- Belief that you will close the deal
- Belief that your products and services will have a positive and profitable effect on your clients after they purchase

YOUR RESULT

When you master these six beliefs, and you are head over heels in love with what you do, your genuine passion for your products and services will be evident to your customer. You'll wake up in the morning more energized, pumped to make connections, pumped to deliver presentations, and excited to sell, and help others. You will exude enthusiasm when you're explaining why prospects need to get on board with your offerings, and why they need to buy. Your positive energy and beliefs will be contagious enough to make sales, gain loyalty, and earn referrals in slightly more, than a New York Minute.

BELIEF IS A CORE SUCCESS VALUE

In high school I sold Cutco knives. I sold them like hotcakes because I believed in my heart that they were the *best* knives on the planet. To this day, I will *still* tell you that they are the best knives on the planet. I still use them. And, I can *still* tell you the 5 reasons why they're the best – but, this isn't a pitch for Cutco knives. It's about my *belief* in Cutco knives.

My belief went so deep, that it has stuck with me for decades. How strongly do you believe in your company? Your products? Yourself? Measure your beliefs on a scale of 1 to 100. With 1 being not so believable to 100 being a forever advocate.

Here's a secret: Your customers feel and measure you and your beliefs on every sales call. If you're a true believer, your customer will become one too, in a New York Minute.

GRAB YOUR IMPLE-MENTOR:
Identify and measure your beliefs.

DO YOU MEASURE
YOURSELF?

No, not your waistline! This is much bigger than that, well, for some of you. I'm referring to how you measure your sales pipeline, your sales productivity line, your sales efficiency line, and your sales training line. These are your sales lifelines.

HERE'S A NEW WAY TO MEASURE:

If you're upset because your sales manager is holding you accountable, it's probably because you're not establishing relationships deep enough to get referred. It's probably because you're not making enough sales to exceed your sales plan quota. It's probably because you're not working hard enough or smart enough to earn your freedom, and it's probably because you're not investing enough time in your own training and personal development.

DO ALL OF THOSE THINGS,
AND YOU'LL BEGIN TO HAVE A BETTER
BOTTOM LINE IN A NEW YORK MINUTE.

SALES IN A NY MINUTE
JENNIFER GLUCKOW

YOUR PAST DICTATES YOUR FUTURE

Your past experiences, your past successes, and your past failures, all create, test, and transform your attitude. Life, business, careers, and family all have their ups, downs, and twists.

Ask yourself: How do you respond to everything that happens to you?

Tell Yourself: Have faith... have faith in yourself... faith that you can be resilient enough to choose your attitude, and change it however needed. **The secret lies in Napoleon Hill's timeless quote:**

"FAITH IS THE HEAD CHEMIST OF THE MIND."

GRAB YOUR IMPLE-MENTOR:

Make a list of your positive past experiences, use them to create your future, and you'll be able to draw on them for even more success in a New York Minute.

HOW IMPORTANT
ARE ETHICS?

Ethics are **everything.** In case you didn't get that, let me repeat it -
ETHICS ARE EVERYTHING

You have three names in your world:
1. One name in life. **2.** One name in sales. **3.** One name online.

And you can choose to do the right thing and maintain a great
reputation, or you can choose to do the wrong thing – either way, it's
your choice, and your reputation.

Some salespeople, and even groups of salespeople have a bad name.
Think about car salespeople. Is your immediate thought positive,
helpful, or negative? An entire industry of salespeople is thought of
negatively because of their sales practices – their ethics. Don't get
Caravana-ed.

HERE'S WHAT TO DO:

Ethics test: Ask yourself, if your grandma were to read about what
you're doing, would she be proud? Maintain your ethics and you'll
be building long-term and long-lasting fruitful relationships in a New
York Minute.

WHAT TO DO IF YOU WITNESS YOUR BOSS DOING THE WRONG THING

Sales can be cutthroat, and sometimes, you may observe a boss or leader who is not doing the right thing. What do you do?

YOU DO THE RIGHT THING NO MATTER WHAT.

Here's the harsh reality: It may mean you need to find a new job.

The bottom line is you gotta do what you feel is right – right for you, right for your customers, right for your colleagues, and right for your company - in that order.

And if your boss is acting unethically, then his/her boss may be involved too.

YOUR ACTION:

Don't follow the wrong footsteps – take the right path and you'll be on the road to success in a New York Minute. #wellsfargo

SALES IN A NY MINUTE
JENNIFER GLUCKOW

WHAT'S YOUR WORK ETHIC?

Growing up, my dad would leave the house every day at 4 AM. He left early so that he could be one of the first people to arrive at his book printing and manufacturing facility. Upon arrival, he made it a point to say "Hi!" to each employee. As the owner, he could have arrived later, but he chose to be there early, and he chose to be the last to leave. That's the kind of work ethic I witnessed my entire life.

HERE'S YOUR PERSONAL "WORK ETHIC" QUIZ:

Are you early for meetings? Are you the last to leave? Are you willing to work whenever there's work to be done?

Start enhancing and improving your work ethic today, and you'll be making more sales in a New York Minute tomorrow - or sooner.

WHAT'S YOUR
WORK ETHIC AND WHERE DID
YOU LEARN IT?

SALES IN A NY MINUTE

JENNIFER GLUCKOW

NOT LUCKY?

My dad says, the harder you work, the luckier you get. Without hard work, you may get lucky here and there, but if you work your ass off, I can promise you that you will begin to be in the right place at the right time, and you will get lucky.

How hard do you work? Hard enough to get lucky?

HERE'S THE SECRET:

It's not just hard work. It's consistent hard work. The habit of working hard will put you in a greater position for more luck.

In sales, the more calls you make, the more prospects you visit, the more sales you attempt, the more "luck" will come your way and you'll be rolling 7s and 11s all the way to the bank, in a New York Minute.

ARE YOU MODELING YOUR
WORK ETHIC AFTER THE
RIGHT PERSON?

SALES IN A NY MINUTE

JENNIFER GLUCKOW

YOU ARE WHERE
YOU WORK

Here's the reality: Many salespeople and entrepreneurs spend their time working from home or in coffee shops. For cheap.

What you may think is "cheap" costs a lot. Poor environment, erratic atmospheres, no business connections, noisy, no networking opportunities, and a stuffy, crowded environment where everyone is lamenting the same situations.

In sales, when you're more productive, you create quality time for better preparation. Better preparation leads to better relationships... better sales presentations...better engagement...and ultimately better (and more) sales.

Your personal success starts with you, your well-being, and your atmosphere. **Here are a few ways to enhance your productivity in your workplace:**

- **Connectivity.** Wifi (fast or else don't even think aboudddit!) and access to an awesome community of people. You're connected with everybody and everything.
- **Natural sunlight brightens (pun intended) your day.** It's mood making and mood enhancing.

- **Coffee.** A must. No if, ands, or (sitting on your) butts. Hook your Keurig up to Death Wish Coffee.
- **Location. Easy to get to.** Near public transportation or short drive to work. Easy to get to other's offices.
- **Clean workspace.** A desk without clutter and without distraction will help you focus on your action items.
- **Greenery. Plants. Flowers.** There's something about greenery that makes you want to relax, breathe, think, and be creative (in that order). Plants are more than eye-pleasing candy. They have a calming effect known to reduce stress and boost your attitude.
- **Healthy.** Having healthy food at your fingertips, and being surrounded by people who frown on potato chips, will make you think twice about reaching your hand into the bag. It will also help trim your waistline. Note: Macarons don't count.
- **Friendly.** This is a given, but make sure you're in a place with happy, friendly people who want to get to know you.

CONNECT: Find a space with a great community of like-minded individuals. Form your own mastermind, inspire and be inspired.
CONNECT: Find a place where you can do business with and refer business to the members. This will make it the ultimate place to work and network.
CO-WORK: Costs more than a coffee, but that's the cost of opportunity.

Did you know that 40% of your adult life is spent working? WHOAH. Your challenge is to find or create a workspace that opens your mind and fills your bank account in a New York Minute.

DO THIS:

Create opportunity. Research co-working spaces in your area. If you travel for work, search for national or global ones. And if you don't have good local co-working options, ask your best customer if they have a spare desk you could rent - hey, seeing them weekly is a good thing!

"

EVERYONE
WANTS TO BE
A BETTER
SALESPERSON
— IN A —
NEW YORK MINUTE.

JENNIFER GLUCKOW
@JENINANYMINUTE

SELLING

ALL ABOUT SELLING...
NEW YORK MINUTE SELLING.

New York City is full. The roads are full. The elevators are full. The restaurants are full. The theatres are full. The subways are full.... Full. It's also full of competitors. And this section is about how to stand out and stand up above the crowd, so that you're seen and perceived *best*.

These minutes are all about the values that you have to possess to:

- Be sales ready (in terms of your customer)
- Make a best first impression last
- Discover the sales details needed to make the sale by asking
- Remove sales excuses from your lexicon
- Get "Your price is too low!" responses
- Rise above sales ruts
- Beat your competition with value not price

AND... MAKE MORE PROFITABLE SALES
IN A NEW YORK MINUTE.

If you implement these minutes, you can add one more full thing to this list: **your wallet**.

5 WAYS TO GET MORE SALES LEADS

I hear salespeople say they don't have enough leads or their leads aren't any good. You ever say that?

Stop blaming. Take responsibility and create your own leads. Yep - it's pretty straightforward. **Create your own leads**.

HERE'S HOW:

1. **Talk to everyone – yes, everyone.** People in the grocery store, at a concert, in the airport, at a restaurant. Talk to everyone. If they're not a lead, they can refer you.
2. **Create your own leads with online attraction.** Start a blog, a YouTube channel, market on Facebook live – go for it. Educate and attract. Join LinkedIn groups and groups in your marketplace and become an active, consistent contributor.
3. **Call your current customers.** See how they're doing – and make sure you provide the same information to them that you're offering online. Check in because you genuinely care, not because you're just trying to make a new sale. The new sale will come when you strengthen the relationship and provide value.

4. **Identify your specific target categories and individuals.** Make a list of the types of people you want to meet and specific people you need to meet with.
5. **Value connect on LinkedIn** by offering free content that your prospect would consider valuable.

Work hard to become attractive, take responsibility and create your own leads and you'll be loaded with a massive pipeline in a New York Minute.

STOP BLAMING.
TAKE RESPONSIBILITY
AND CREATE
YOUR OWN LEADS.

JENNIFER GLUCKOW
@JENINANYMINUTE

SALES IN A NY MINUTE
JENNIFER GLUCKOW

NETWORKING, COLD CALLING AND SOCIAL MEDIA, OH MY!

You want to make more sales - of course you do. Whether it's for your quota, your business, your side hustle, or for your new idea. The question is, how? Do you knock on doors or do you go another route? How do you find new leads? Potential customers? Potential referrers?

There are *too many* options and tools for salespeople and there are *too many* experts who will tell you to do it one way or the other. Some experts say, "Cold calling is dead." Others say, "It's ALIVE!"

HERE ARE THE REAL ANSWERS:

Spammy cold calls are dead. And spammy emails are dead. But cold calling is not dead. Cold emails are not dead if they're targeted.

I know so many people who have built their business and their relationships by cold calling - meeting strangers who turned into customers, one at a time. Now, is it the most effective way? Let's argue that in another minute.

"THE MORE BALLS YOU THROW UP IN THE AIR, THE MORE WILL COME POURING DOWN INTO YOUR BANK ACCOUNT."

JENNIFER GLUCKOW
@JENINANYMINUTE

This is true only if you have the right targets and use social and business tools to connect. Use the phone after you connect on LinkedIn (yes, make "connected" cold calls), connect digitally (email and social media), and of course, participate in face-to-face networking.

The trifecta combo will win you more visibility, connections, and sales in a New York Minute.

HERE'S WHAT TO DO:

Create a time investment plan with the trifecta approach. Allocate time for networking, time for cold calling, and time for digital selling. Figure out where the majority of your customers hang out the most and spend the most time there.

"

DRINK MORE
COFFEE
with more people
MORE OFTEN
— AND —
MAKE MORE SALES!

Be social offline as much as you are online.

JENNIFER GLUCKOW
@JENINANYMINUTE

SALES IN A NY MINUTE
JENNIFER GLUCKOW

IT'S ALL ABOUT
GETTING THE APPOINTMENT

Your trifecta approach to prospecting should have one goal: **get the appointment.**

It's not just about making the sale, it's about getting the appointment so you can connect over coffee and build a relationship. Whether or not you build a relationship has a direct effect on whether or not you will close the sale.

And here's the vital piece: the prospect must believe there is value in meeting with you or they won't want to continue the conversation, let alone meet.

DO THIS:

Ask questions that engage them. Ask questions that show your genuine interest in helping them succeed. Give ideas and strategies that help them profit and win. If you lead your conversations with ideas that will help THEM, they'll be asking YOU for the appointment in a New York Minute.

WHY CONNECT?

You're kidding, right?

People do business with people they like.
Think about the people you do business with. Like 'em?

I've built my business through networking and so will you. Whether you work for an established company, or you're starting your own business, or you're a veteran in sales, or a sales newbie, networking is critical to your success.

Think about your list of contacts. Is it a database or a sales tool? Your contact list is the ultimate sales tool - one that's current and growing.

DO THIS:

Find networking meetings in your area. Visit a bunch and determine which would be a good fit for you. Join one or two where you can make a great impact and make lifelong friends (and customers).

MESSAGE
→

"

MEET NEW PEOPLE,
MAKE

NEW

FRIENDS,
KEEP OLD FRIENDSHIPS,
AND LEARN
EVERYONE'S NEEDS.

JENNIFER GLUCKOW
@JENINANYMINUTE

THE 11 VALUES
OF NETWORKING

Building your connections will connect the dots to the sale. Here's the value of networking and connecting.

VALUE 1. MEET NEW PEOPLE.

The obvious might not be so obvious. You meet people of influence, of importance to your business, and people that you can do business with. The key is to make it a continuous process, and networking is both the easiest and best path to make "meeting" happen.

VALUE 2. INCREASE CONNECTIONS.

Your connections can (and are more than willing to) make introductions to new connections. And, by making an introduction, they will help you build new connections, with more trust, faster than you could if you cold called and had to build your reputation, credibility, and reliability from scratch.

VALUE 3. GAIN ACCESS TO PEOPLE AND INFORMATION.

People come to networking events and trade shows that might not otherwise be available to you. And not just people, connecting also gives you access to feedback and advice that you may not be privy to otherwise. Access to new ideas. Access to industry information. And access to people. Networking access is powerful.

VALUE 4. GAIN MORE PROSPECTS.

Meaningful engagement leads to quality (not necessarily qualified) prospects. Keep it light at the networking meeting, and schedule coffee for a closer look and more relevant talk.

VALUE 5. BUILD YOUR REPUTATION.

If you offer consistent valuable information, and take consistent valuable actions over an extended period of time, you will build your reputation, and others will come to trust you, do business with you, and refer you.

VALUE 6. INCREASE BUSINESS.

More connections. More engagement. More conversations. More ideas. More introductions. More leads. More appointments. More sales. Got it?

VALUE 7. INCREASE PROFIT.

Your cost of acquisition becomes the time it takes staying in touch with your network. This is always less than the cost to advertise. Plus word of mouth referrals often result in quicker sales than non-referral business. And increased profit because increased sales through referrals are less likely to hammer price.

VALUE 8. ADVANCE YOUR CAREER.

Find a new job or internal promotion. Find a meaningful contact or
even a mentor. Making a networking connection can lead you to a job.

VALUE 9. ACCELERATE YOUR SUCCESS.

Networking will accelerate your learning curve and your professional
development. By networking with people across a variety of industries,
you will gain new and valuable information. New information that can
make a tremendous difference in your business and impact your sales.
For example, one of my networking groups has a business banker, a
CPA, a social media expert, an SEO expert, a local marketing expert,
a web design expert (and more!). After meeting with each person, I
always walk away with a page full of notes, ideas, and strategies to fuel
my business. Yes I refer them, yes they refer me, but in the middle is
an incredible information exchange.

VALUE 10. MAKE LIFELONG FRIENDS.

You can gain lifelong friends networking. Some say you become who
you associate yourself with, or at least you are measured by who you
associate yourself with. I say, associate yourself with those you would
want to be stuck on a deserted island with. Seek smart, ambitious,
friendly and credible people and you'll be fortunate to make lifelong
friends while networking.

VALUE 11. BUILD YOUR OWN BRAND
AND YOUR OWN COMMUNITY.

Creating a network community where you are known, liked, trusted,
respected, and referred takes time. It does not happen in a New

York Minute. The key is to stay visible and valuable - consistently. Demonstrate your knowledge reliability, and leadership ability. Show testimonials. And most important - GIVE. Givers get more than takers.

For more Values of Networking, go to salesinanyminutebook.com/networking and download your free networking eBook.

"

"NETWORKING LEADS TO **MEETING**,
LEADS TO **ENGAGING**,
LEADS TO **SALES**,
LEADS TO **MONEY**,
LEADS TO **RELATIONSHIPS**,
LEADS TO **MORE SALES**,
LEADS TO **MORE MONEY**,
LEADS TO **TESTIMONIALS**,
LEADS TO **REFERRALS**,
LEADS TO **EVEN MORE SALES**,
LEADS TO **EVEN MORE MONEY**."

JENNIFER GLUCKOW
@JENINANYMINUTE

SALES IN A NY MINUTE
JENNIFER GLUCKOW

THE DIFFERENCE BETWEEN NETWORKING AND TARGETED NETWORKING

Picture this: You're in a room full of people at a networking event wanting to make connections. And you, as a salesperson or entrepreneur, want to make as many connections as you possibly can. Correct? No. That would be incorrect. What you want to do is to have pre-selected three or four targets who can make the most impact to your sales, your connections, or your career, and make certain that you invest your networking time with them. No sales presentation, no "here's what I do," or "here's how I help other people," rather, have value-based conversations with them and about them that lead to the next meeting. A casual coffee or a casual lunch, so that you can deepen the conversation or the relationship.

DO THIS:

Review the attendee list prior to your next networking event and pre-select the people you want to meet. Research them, connect with them on LinkedIn (with a personalized message), find out what they're posting and what they care about so that when you do meet them, you'll find common ground and build rapport way faster.

❝

CONTRARY TO POPULAR BELIEF, NETWORKING IS NOT ABOUT NUMBERS.

. . . .

NETWORKING IS ABOUT TARGETING.

. . . .

WHEN YOU TARGET THE RIGHT PEOPLE
AT THE RIGHT EVENTS, YOU MAKE CONNECTIONS,
BUILD RAPPORT, AND CREATE RELATIONSHIP
OPPORTUNITIES THAT ULTIMATELY MAKE
SALES AND LIFELONG FRIENDSHIPS
IN A NEW YORK MINUTE.

JENNIFER GLUCKOW
@JENINANYMINUTE

SALES IN A NY MINUTE
JENNIFER GLUCKOW

YOU HAD ME AT HELLO!

Face-to-face impressions are the most powerful. With a sharp look, a huge smile, a firm handshake and a warm greeting, you can create an immediate favorable impression. One that you can build on and one that will lead to a relaxed, engaging conversation.

ASK YOURSELF:

How sharp is your look?
How huge is your smile?
How firm is your handshake?
How warm is your greeting?

If you're not at 100% on each one, you will lose your first impression in a New York second. And the sale, in less than a New York Minute.

SALES IN A NY MINUTE
JENNIFER GLUCKOW

THE SECRET TO SMART NETWORKING

If you want to make more meaningful, powerful, and lucrative networking connections, **here's the three-part secret:**

FIRST

Go where your customers and prospects go, and get involved. Be seen and known as a leader, not just a member.

SECOND

Go where the people in the group do business with people you want to do business with. Meet as many as you can, and exchange quality information. Not just a sales pitch.

THIRD

Go where the people in the group are positive and willing to give as much (or more) than they wanna take. Give to them first, show them your value. This is how I network, and it works. If you immerse yourself in these kinds of networking groups, get involved and take value-driven actions with these kinds of people, more connections and more sales will be yours in a New York Minute.

TOTAL
NETWORKING

Many people save networking for official networking meetings. NO! Not you, right?

Network opportunities are everywhere...and anywhere. You network at parties, out with existing customers, on airplanes, in seminars, even at trade shows...Don't you? I've built my business by networking, making connections, making appointments, and ultimately making sales that lead to relationships and word-of-mouth referrals.

HERE'S WHAT TO DO:

Talk to everyone you can, and make a friendly favorable impression. Make the person you're talking to *want* to continue the conversation, make them *want* to meet later for coffee. By being more outgoing, more friendly, making others feel good, smiling, and making the effort to proactively network with others at each and every opportunity you get, you will become relaxed and more well known in a New York Minute.

Go to *salesinanyminute.com/57* and get my eBook with 57 places to network that go beyond business cards and weak leads to referrals and new business.

LOOK SHARP
NETWORKING

Imagine you just ran into your best customer at a networking event. How do you want to look? Me? I always try to look my best.

**I DRESS WITH STYLE
TO IMPRESS WITH
MY "LOOK" FIRST, ENGAGE
WITH FRIENDLINESS
TO CONNECT SECOND,
AND THEN IMPRESS WITH
MY BRAIN, THIRD.**

MAKE IT COUNT:

Your new customer could be right in front of you. And your job is to be ready to attract with your look, your friendliness, and your brain. Impressive attraction equals more leads, more connections, and ultimately more sales – all in a New York Minute.

SALES IN A NY MINUTE
JENNIFER GLUCKOW

WRITE ON BUSINESS CARDS
TO MAKE MORE SALES

Ever taken a business card out of your briefcase and tried to remember who gave it to you? And then, two weeks later, you end up throwing the card away because you can't remember? That's because you failed to write anything ON the card to remind you.

The secret is: Write a note on the card you receive one second after you finish your meeting, so that you can follow up and make that sale in a New York Minute.

YOUR ACTION:

Review the business cards that you recently received and write down everything you can remember about each person. Use a CRM or an Excel spreadsheet to store information about prospects and customers. Make a date to follow up - even if it's just to say "Hi" or send something of value. Staying in touch with value is just as important as making the initial connection.

"
"ARE YOUR BUSINESS CARDS
KEPT OR THROWN AWAY?"

▙▙

EVER WONDER WHAT

PEOPLE
WILL WRITE
ABOUT YOU
ON YOUR
BUSINESS CARD?

JENNIFER GLUCKOW
@JENINANYMINUTE

REALITY: NETWORKING IS MORE THAN A STACK OF CARDS

How many business cards do you get (collect) when networking? "Lots." How many of those turn into real appointments? "Less than lots." How many of those turn into sales? "Not enough."

MAJOR CHALLENGE:

What is your present strategy to meet new people, get engaged, get their card (or connect online), and turn their connection into money? "Ouch!"

These strategies will help you select the best meetings to attend and the best groups to join:

- Match your selection of the event or group with the probability of a prospect becoming a sale or the probability of gaining a quality referral.
- Match your time allocation with the potential value of the meeting. How much time do you need to invest in the group to make it "worth" your time?
- Match the attendees with your present customers. How many of your customers are in the room? Think about joining a meeting where you'll be seeing your present customers often and remain top of mind.

- Evaluate the group for givers and getters. Join a group of givers, and hopefully you're a giver too, so you'll fit right in.
- Intensify your focus. Be present. Be valuable. Focus your attention on how you and the others in the group can win. That's the right group.

GRAB YOUR IMPLE-MENTOR
I'll walk you through how to do this.

AND ONE MORE ACTION:

Hopefully you've already downloaded my 57 Varieties of the Best Networking Opportunities eBook. If not, you can get it here: *salesinanyminute.com/57* . Study it. Check the most powerful places. Take notes as you read. And, select the five places that you want to go, and the five places where your customers currently go, and start there.

NETWORK WITH A STRATEGY AND TURN YOUR STACK OF CARDS INTO A STACK OF SALES IN A NEW YORK MINUTE.

SALES IN A NY MINUTE
JENNIFER GLUCKOW

CONSISTENT PRE-CALL RESEARCH

I overheard a sales conversation in which the prospect asked the salesperson, "Do you know what I do? Did you look me up before you cold called me?" And the rep stuttered, "uh...." while frantically googling the prospect's company.

Think he won that sale? He didn't even make it past the prospect's first question.

Caution: Going in without pre-call research is sales embarrassment that leads to sales death.

Research is so easy today. Google and LinkedIn the prospect you're about to meet with or speak to. Understand the other person before you walk in the door or pick up the phone by doing as much research as possible. Research you can use to understand what they do, discover common ground, and develop questions based on what you've learned. I'll give examples of good questions in another minute.

YOUR ACTION:

Open your sales routine with consistent pre-call research and you'll be closing more sales in a New York Minute.

JENNIFER GLUCKOW

SALES PREPARATION PART 1

Get ready. Get set. Get more ready!

The hardest part is "get ready." In sales, it's known as "preparation."

If asked, most salespeople, if not all, would say they know preparation is important. But most salespeople (not you, of course) are not preparing the right way for meetings, potential sales calls, or networking events.

HERE'S HOW TO PREPARE:

- Prepare in terms of THEM.
- Ask your friends if they know someone or something about your potential customer. If you have a good circle, the likelihood is somebody knows somebody.
- Make a short slide deck that clarifies your ideas.
- Keep thinking about it and document thoughts immediately.

Being ready, communicating and presenting with excellence and personalized interaction, leads to a memorable sales and networking experience - and the sale - in a New York Minute.

SALES IN A NY MINUTE
JENNIFER GLUCKOW

SALES PREPARATION PART 2

Here's what to prepare so when you meet with your customer, you're ready for the sale:

PREPARATION A: ATTITUDE.

You need the right attitude **all the time** to win the sale. And for most people (especially if you grew up or live in NYC) that attitude is not natural – it's something you need to work on **every** day. The key is consistency.

PREPARATION B: BE BRIEF AND BELIEVABLE.

Tell your story – how you, your company, your products and services *help* your customer. Be brief or they'll lose interest. To be brief, you need to practice. And to be believable you need to believe.

PREPARATION C: CUSTOMER CONNECTION.

10 years ago, making a customer connection was harder than today. With social selling, the information you need to make a customer connection is at your fingertips...literally. All you need to do is Google them! Before your meeting, use Google, their website, their blog, and social media, especially LinkedIn, to find out what's important about *them* and to *them*.

PREPARATION D: MEET WITH THE DECISION MAKER.

Whether or not you're meeting with the decision-maker (and I *hope* you are), be prepared as if the decision-maker will walk into the room.

PREPARATION E: ENGAGEMENT AND ENTHUSIASM.

The best way to engage is to be prepared with questions, information and ideas about *them*, that both demonstrate you've done your research, and make them stop and think, and respond in terms of you.

PREPARATION F: FOCUS. FRIENDLY. FIND THE MOTIVE.

Focus on the meeting outcome. Create dialogue and interactions to get you there. Be as friendly as you can be without losing your sincerity. And uncover, through questions (Preparation E), why they want to buy. Their "why" is your answer to "when" and "urgency."

PREPARATION G: GIVE VALUE.

The only way to do that is to figure out what the prospect perceives valuable. If you think you're providing value and the customer does not perceive it to be, then it's not value. Value is NOT a "proposition" – it's an offering that helps them in their effort to succeed.

PREPARATION H.

If you're not prepared enough at the end of Preparation G to make the sale, then you will certainly need Preparation H. **Symptom:** You're sitting at your desk too much and need to get off your ass and get to work.

Now you have all the ways to prepare. Go make a sale in a New York Minute.

SALES IN A NY MINUTE
JENNIFER GLUCKOW

READY RULES!

Ready to make the sale? Maybe. Get research-ready. The key word to research-ready is "online." What kind of online research do you do before a sales call? Do you read all about your prospect and their company online? Did you check out *all* of their social media accounts and postings online? Not just what they're tweeting about, but what's being said about them - online. Reputation-ready and research-ready gets you prepared to engage with real-world information.

REALITY:

As much research as you do about the prospect, your prospective customer is likely to have done more – about you. What they find when they Google you, determines your fate. Become searchable and findable and you'll become valuable enough to make all kinds of sales in a New York Minute.

BUY YOURNAME.COM RIGHT NOW.
MAKE A SIMPLE WEBSITE ABOUT WHO YOU ARE
AND WHAT YOU OFFER YOUR CLIENTS
- HOW YOU HELP THEM.

Link your social platforms to your site. If you're not active on social media, start with LinkedIn, Facebook, Twitter, Instagram and YouTube and depending on your business, Pinterest. Create a content calendar for daily value messaging. Track your ratio of sales posts to value posts. How well do you measure up? Set Google alerts on your name, your company name, and on your competition.

VALUE MESSAGING
AND SOCIAL PROOF
GENERATE
INBOUND CALLS.

EARN TESTIMONIALS
(WRITTEN AND VIDEO)
FROM YOUR CUSTOMERS.
POST PROOF ONLINE.

HERE'S THE HARSH REALITY:

You can say you're great (otherwise known as bragging), but no one cares when you say it. When other people say you're great or that your products and services are great, then prospects will call.

HOW TO MAKE YOUR BEST IMPRESSION

People say that first impressions are made within 7 seconds. I say first impressions are made waaay before that. Your prospect has sized you up *before* you've even met. They've Googled you. Just like you've Googled them.

Consider this: Five seconds after they Google you, their first impression is set.

WHAT WILL YOUR PROSPECT FIND?
HOW GOOGLE-IMPRESSIVE ARE YOU?

Google yourself right now and see. OUCH! Is there enough to want to buy from you? Here's the new first-impression reality. You must create an online presence that's so stellar, people can't wait to meet you. How? Your imperative is to create an online presence and reputation that makes an *impressive* impression.

- Create a blog where you post value messages.
- Create a weekly podcast that your followers can't wait to listen to.
- Generate an impressive following on social media by offering helpful and valuable ideas.

YOU ONLY HAVE ONE CHANCE TO MAKE A BEST PRE-IMPRESSION, A SOCIAL IMPRESSION, A VALUE IMPRESSION, AND YOU MAKE IT IN WAY LESS THAN A NEW YORK MINUTE.

MAKE IT HAPPEN:

Start now. Social media, blogging, videos, and podcasting are the NOW! opportunity. Nike says, "Just do it!" I say, "Just do it *now*." If you like written communication, start with a blog. More verbal? Start with a video blog or podcast. Create a lineup of guests/experts/ potential clients/industry leaders and ask each one if they'll interview with you. Then, create great content that your prospects want more of. Publish, share, and engage! Impress yourself and you're certain to impress others.

BUILD YOUR ONLINE PRESENCE, YOUR SOCIAL PRESENCE. YOUR VALUE MESSAGES.

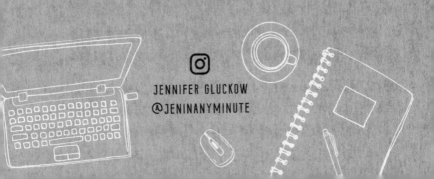

JENNIFER GLUCKOW
@JENINANYMINUTE

HERE'S MY NUMBER, SO CALL ME...MAYBE?

No one likes to cold call. But because you need new business, it seems like the only path. **Update:** That was true 20 years ago – but not today. The path to new leads is way easier today. Attraction and social media have become the new way to sell, and the new path to attract.

Ask yourself: What are you doing to get prospects to call you? What are you posting that interests them? When a prospect calls you, they have done their own research – they've Googled you, they've asked people they know and trust if they've done business with you, and they've researched your competition. Is your social media presence valuable enough to create an inbound call?

TAKE ACTION:

Build your online presence, your social presence, and your value messages. Read all of your social postings then ask yourself, would you respond to this? Where's your social proof? When faced with a need and a choice, your online presence will help your prospects make the decision to call you in a New York Minute.

STATE OF CURRENT YIELDS CURRENCY

Years ago when you were looking for your pager or Blackberry, you'd give up after searching for about a minute or two. Fast forward a decade. Can you imagine being without your iPhone? What's your state of current, and how are you turning new technology into currency?

TO BE ADEPT IN SALES, YOU MUST ADOPT IN TECHNOLOGY. AND GET TO "TAKE FULL ADVANTAGE" MASTERY.

TAKE ACTION:

As soon as something new comes out, how quick are you to take on the new technology? Buy it, use it, master it, save time with it, and stay current.

And here's a trick: if you sell your old technology right before the newer model comes out, you can get top dollar for it making your new investment less. Invest in new. Invest in now. And your customers will be investing in you.

Your life is no different than your customer's business life. And they expect current from you in a New York Minute.

SELLING · PREPARATION

SALES IN A NY MINUTE
JENNIFER | GLUCKOW

SOCIAL
SELLING DEFINED

Here's the strategic side of social selling and exactly what you need to do, to get people to buy.

- **Rule no. 1.** Stop pushing socially and start attracting.
- **Rule no. 2.** Stop spamming, also known as e-mail blasting, to an audience that doesn't know you.
- **Rule no. 3.** Start with your best customers and prospects and deliver messages that they both perceive as valuable and might be willing to act on...and pass on to someone else.

Social selling begins with your consistent value messaging and your sales offerings, and it ends with the reputation that's searchable and then immediately findable. When people find you and they perceive that you're likable, valuable and safe, then they're willing to socially engage and ultimately buy.

HERE'S THE REALITY:

There's no such thing as a "one-call close" in social selling. Just because they hit the like button doesn't mean they love you enough or trust you enough to hit the share button. Or even the buy now button - that requires trust and proof.

I like it...I like it...I like it. I believe it. I'll buy it. The key to winning social sales is for your followers to share, retweet or forward your valuable messages. Keep in mind, all of these elements of social selling are free!

YOU'RE FREE TO EITHER
TAKE ADVANTAGE
OF SOCIAL SELLING AND BE A

SOCIAL ROCKSTAR

OR YOU COULD LOOK LIKE
AN ASS
WITH NO SOCIAL SKILLS
IN A VIRTUAL
NEW YORK MINUTE.

JENNIFER GLUCKOW
@JENINANYMINUTE

SALES IN A NY MINUTE
JENNIFER GLUCKOW

FROM ONLINE TO ON-THE-MONEY,
IT'S ALL ABOUT THE SEES AND THE C'S

The power of online is the ability to connect with people who live all over the world and have the potential to be customers, friends, mentors, and referral partners. But, most people leave the conversation online and don't convert their connection into sales.

Here are the 9 New York Minute C's you need to complete to turn your online relationships from strangers to genuine connections, and begin converting and closing more sales in a New York Minute:

1. **Commit.** Commit to investing in the power of online. The potential is real. If you commit, then you need to dedicate time daily to building relationships. And I am talking about real relationships - not merely gain followers or follow others.

2. **Create and Contribute.** Create engaging, unique and helpful content, and contribute with value daily. What are you putting out that others can benefit from? Think articles, blogs, podcasts, videos - content people can profit from, learn from or do better from. Don't just share other people's trending articles. Be the thought leader.

3. **Connect with Comments and Conversation.** Form real connections by commenting, conversing, and having meaningful

dialogue. This is not just hitting the like button - it's commenting why you liked something or why something inspires you. It's sharing other people's posts.

4. **Your Connection's Connections.** There is massive power in your ability to connect with your connection's connections. It's no longer about just having your own set of connections, it's about figuring out which connections of yours have connections you want to connect with. Think back to the rolodex... (If you were born after I was, a rolodex is a small file box that sat on business people's desks. They used to add their contacts' business cards and it had a rotating mechanism so you could flip through the cards. Old school, I know.) With a rolodex you had access to one set of connections - your own. Now, the power no longer lies in who you know or who knows you. It's about who you know and who *they* know.

5. **Call or grab Coffee!** *Yep, coffee!* You can now have coffee with anyone anywhere in the world. All you need to do is grab a cup of joe (hopefully it's Deathwish Coffee) and plan a Facetime or Zoom meeting. Both phone and coffee meetings require prep and real conversation - this is where the magic, eh, real connections form (notice you're online, but still face to face.)

6. **Convert (or close the sale!).** Just like people you meet in person, not everyone will convert, but the more people you have coffee conversations with, the more will convert to real connections, real relationships and sales.

7. **Cash or Credit Card.** You do know how to collect it, right? Be ready when someone wants to buy.

8. **Celebrate.** *Celebrate the sale.* Celebrate the connection. It seems nothing is real anymore unless it's posted online so be sure to post a selfie with your newfound friend.

9. **The final C is Clarity of Vision.** Your ability to see what opportunities are in front of you and take action.

SOCIAL MEDIA DO'S, DON'TS, ALWAYS AND NEVERS

Social media has incredible tools that can help you access a network of people near and far away who you may not otherwise have had access to. Connections that help you build relationships and make sales.

Here are the rules to follow (many are unwritten until now):

DO'S

- Do comment on strangers' posts.
- Do share value messages.
- Do spend a minimum of 15 minutes a day engaging with other people's posts.
- Do be genuine, be yourself, open up.
- Do respond and engage to others' posts.
- Do address negative comments (if there are any!)
- Do use video to connect with your audience.

DON'TS

- Don't connect with someone for the sole purpose of trying to sell them.

- Don't connect with someone and then try to sell them. Build a relationship first!
- Don't post more sales messages than value messages.
- Don't give to get (just give to give).

ALWAYS

- Always consider your social media time an investment - don't get caught up in other people's drama.
- Always have a plan - a consistent social content calendar.
- Always have social goals - it's not just about the number of followers. What's more important is their engagement and your growth.
- Always make certain you consider your reputation each time you post or comment.

NEVERS

- Never get political or religious.
- Never be creepy...seriously.
- Never get into an argument online.

"WHAT GOES ON SOCIAL,
STAYS ON SOCIAL!"

JENNIFER GLUCKOW
@JENINANYMINUTE

SALES PITCH OR PODCAST? WHICH ONE IS WORTHLESS?

Still relying on a sales pitch to make the sale? Seriously? You need way more than a pitch. You need a podcast.

Here's why:

- **Your prospects will get to know you** - the real you. They'll see your human side. And they'll determine if they like you and trust you. So many people who I meet for the first time tell me, "Jen, I listen to you on *Sell or Die* and I feel like I know you!" And then they ask a question about something that's just happened in my life, like a trip or a seminar, or something personal because they heard me speak about it on the show. Then I have this moment of, "Wow, you do know me!"
- **It's one-sided rapport-building that works.** Well, that's as long as you're likeable and make the effort to get to know them too.
- **You can tell stories** that demonstrate your knowledge, expertise and service. Build the trust factor.
- **You can get guests on your show** who drop a line about how great it is working with you or using your product - testimonials that are unprompted. Testimonials that are genuine (so long as you deserve them).

- **You can get in the door with a CEO** or decision-maker by interviewing them to showcase their expertise. Would a CEO rather join you to hear your product pitch or provide their expertise and knowledge and gain notoriety on your podcast?
- **People actually listen to podcasts** all the way through. Don't just trust me, trust the stats. The stats say so.
- **Friends tell their friends about podcasts** - talk about word of mouth!
- **Strangers will find you easily** through search (if your topic is a good one).
- **It takes multiple exposures and different mediums** to get your message through. Expose yourself multiple times. But don't be medium, be rare and well-done.

DO THIS FIRST: GRAB YOUR IMPLE-MENTOR

Some things to consider:

- What will your show be about?
- Will it be an interview-based show or a host talk show? (I recommend interviews for salespeople and entrepreneurs).
- How often will it air?
- How will you get the word out?
- How will you monetize it?
- If you need help, contact me. We have a course on it.

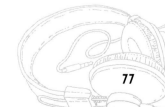

MAKE YOUR PODCAST A
HIT IN A NEW YORK MINUTE

You and I are used to *instant*. Instant coffee, instant response, instant action, instant service, and instant gratification.

Do you want to create a podcast that's an instant hit?

Here's what to do:

TECH

You'll need the basics. Mic, headphones, recording and editing software and publishing software. More on this here: *resources.sellordiepodcast.com*.

FORMAT

Solo or interview show? Try both.
Listen to other podcasts. As you listen, make a list of what you like and what you don't like. That should become your do and don't do list!

BROADCAST

Consistency and content are critical. Let your listeners know what to expect and then put a show out on the same day and same time every week. If you're good, people will rely on your edu-tainment (education entertainment) and it can't be haphazard. Say something valuable and subscribable.

Get ahead. Record the first 5 episodes before launch and stay ahead.

CONTENT

Value, Value, Value. I cannot say content enough. Give people a reason to want to listen. As with all content you offer, think about how you can deliver value messages through your podcast. Who are your ideal listeners? What would they want to learn? What would inspire them? What would keep them coming back for more, or better yet, hit that subscribe button? Or even better, tell others?

GROWTH

Create shareable bytes. What would make your listeners want to share it with a friend, colleague, or family member?

Promote on social media to your followers and have your guests promote to their followers.

The key to growth is getting good ratings, reviews and subscribers.

MONETIZE

Podcasting is fun, and it's even more fun when you're making money.

Ads are one form of revenue. MAJOR REVENUE will come from guests and listeners who you turn into customers. Get your listeners off the pod and onto your list.

Create a scalable, shareable, hit podcast and you'll be earning more dough, creating more connections, and improving your notoriety in a New York Minute.

P.S. IF YOU WANT HELP.
CONTACT SELLORDIE@GITOMER.COM.

SALES IN A NY MINUTE
JENNIFER GLUCKOW

DISCOVER YOUR OUT-FIT

As a child you were taught to fit in.
In school. In family. In fashion (your outfit). And of course, socially.

Not too tall, not too short, not too thin, not too fat, not too loud, you know, be in. Fit in.

As a kid, you learned it as, the Goldilocks syndrome: "just right."

IN SALES AND BUSINESS, THE PHILOSOPHY IS
THE OPPOSITE. AND YOUR ENTIRE PROCESS
MUST BE RE-LEARNED AND REDONE.
YOU NEED TO STAND OUT.

If you fit in, you'll drown in a sea of competition, and no one will see you as different or better than others. Not only that, but because you're kinda like others you'll lose sales on price like everyone else does.

Attracting prospects, buyers, customers, and connections is about being friendly, offering value, and differentiating yourself from your competition. In short, *not* fitting in.

GRAB YOUR IMPLE-MENTOR:
Differentiate yourself.

Do this fit-ness exam and ask yourself:

- What makes you attractive?
- What value do you offer the marketplace?
- How noticeable are you?
- What do people think and say when they see you or your message?
- What makes you different from your competition?
- What makes you unique?
- What makes you memorable?
- What makes your customers want to spread the word?
- Why do your present customers return time after time?
  (or maybe they don't)
- What is your customer's perceived value of your differentiation?

ONCE YOU HAVE THE ANSWERS,
COMMUNICATE THEM THROUGH
YOUR CONVERSATIONS WITH
PROSPECTS, CUSTOMERS, AND
ON YOUR SOCIAL CHANNELS,
AND WATCH YOUR SALES STAND
OUT IN A NEW YORK MINUTE.

SALES IN A NY MINUTE
JENNIFER GLUCKOW

DISCOVERING YOUR
BUSINESS OUT-FIT

Do customers and prospects care about the features and benefits that make you different, or do they really want the value you offer that helps them succeed?

Note: If you think customers don't care, then your "differentiators" don't matter! Offer something different, something that's valued by your buyers.

HERE ARE SOME PLACES WHERE YOU NEED TO STAND OUT:

Online - Is your site ready to do business? Easy to navigate? Easy to buy? Responsive? Designed to help? Built-in SEO that makes you searchable and findable? Does anyone say WOW after they visit? Your dynamic website is no longer an option. Review your site quarterly and make updates that keep it fresh and standing out.

On Email - Your language, your tone, your humor, your images all give you an opportunity to stand out. WOW your customers with content they want to read and want to share. Make it so good that they want to share it with other prospects and even your competition! It's all about your subject line, your open rate and your clickthrough rate.

In Networking Groups - I used to lead a weekly networking meeting in NYC . The people who got noticed, most spoken with after the meeting, and got the most business, were the ones who gave funny and memorable commercials. They stood out. I used to create something dynamic, engaging and memorable EVERY week. The key is to prep ahead of time, practice your pitch and deliver an outstanding commercial. Do you?

In Service - How quickly do you respond? Answer with a live (friendly) human being? 24-7? Want a service report card? Your business Facebook page, yelp, and online reputation will tell the tale.

Ever experience service that was so good that you just had to tell your friends?

HERE ARE SOME REAL EXAMPLES:

- When Zappos offered free delivery both ways - they stood out.
- When Amazon created free two-day shipping (okay, almost free, prime users) - they stood out.
- Hertz rental car in Miami will meet elite customers at baggage claim, help you with your bags, and bring your rental to the terminal when you're ready.

When you experience service like this, it will inspire you to take your service from great to WOW.

What do you do to make your customers say, "WOW"?

HOW DO YOU STAND OUT?

Do this fit-ness exercise: Visit the sites of your five most hated competitors. Who wows? Who wins? I hope you do. Determine your difference. Refine your offer. Communicate your value. Create your market attraction. Invest in wow. And bank the business in a New York Minute.

DO YOU SELF-ASSESS
OR SECOND GUESS??

When you get rejected, how do you take it? Do you get pissed off? Do you second guess yourself – shoulda, woulda, coulda? Or, do you sit down with yourself and go over what actually happened? And then decide what you're going to do better next time?

Here's the secret: the best self-assessment tool in the world is right in your pocket. It's your smartphone. If you make a habit of hitting the record button each time you make a sales presentation, and then play it back after you leave, you will immediately hear and understand what went right and what went wrong. You will immediately hear and understand what you need to do better next time.

OUTCOME:

LISTENING TO YOUR OWN SALES PRESENTATION WILL NOT ONLY HELP YOU GET BETTER IN A NEW YORK MINUTE. IT WILL SHOW YOU YOUR STRENGTHS AND WEAKNESSES. YOUR PROWESS AND YOUR FLAWS IN A NEW YORK SECOND.

SALES IN A NY MINUTE
JENNIFER GLUCKOW

AND THE MORAL
OF THE STORY IS...

When you're meeting with a customer, most of your sales presentation should be centered around asking the prospect about them, finding out their emotional reason for purchase, and helping them see the value of purchasing from you.

When it's time to talk about your products and services, incorporate as much storytelling throughout your presentation as possible. Over time this will develop a long-term relationship with them.

Here's why you should be telling stories, not pitching:
- Stories are more engaging. Once upon a time...
- They create better listening opportunities - people WANT to hear the end
- They're more memorable than facts and figures

Stories create an emotional connection and an emotional response. People buy based on emotion not logic. If your story creates the right emotional connection, it can trigger the sale.

THE MORAL OF THE STORY IS:

Use stories to close more sales in a New York Minute. And you all will live happily ever after.

WORKING TIME
HINT: IT'S NOT 9-5

Most sales are made before 9AM and after 5PM. In B to B sales, even in B to C sales, they're not made during the standard work day. Between 9 and 5, most people are busy working, not buying. Decision-makers are responding to emails, putting out fires, coaching their teams, and following up with clients and prospects – they're focused on *their* business, not *yours*. Consumers are also working, waiting to get home to shop online. People work from 9 to 5, but before 9 and after 5, their wallets are open.

What's your strategy for meeting with B to B prospects? Your coffee-drinking, money-making routine should start before 9 with a customer or prospect. In B to C, your online presence should be ready 24/7/365. The new 9 to 5.

HERE'S WHAT TO DO:

By meeting with your prospects in a casual, relaxed place, by being online and ready to sell 24/7, you can help empty their wallets in a cash, check or credit card New York Minute.

SALES IN A NY MINUTE
JENNIFER GLUCKOW

THE TRUTH IN SALES
LEADS TO MORE SALES

In high school I worked in a neighborhood clothing boutique. On day one, my manager said, "Don't force anything. If something doesn't look good on someone else, find them something that does look good. Don't let anyone go home with something that doesn't look amazing."

At first, this seemed contrary to selling - wasn't I supposed to sell the most clothing possible (and thereby make more commission?). Isn't that why they hired me? To sell?

After helping a few customers, and following my manager's strict instructions, it hit me. If the customer went home with something that didn't look good and their spouse or friends, their "trusted advisors" said, "Ew, return it," they would never trust me (or shop with me again). But, if they got the, "Oooh la la" response, they would be back in a New York Minute. And bring their friends.

HERE'S THE LESSON:

Tell the truth. Make a friend. Become a trusted advisor and you win. Think long term, not just right now. Your job as a salesperson is to help the client and you'll be making more sales in a New York Minute.

SALES IN A NY MINUTE

JENNIFER GLUCKOW

SHOW ME THE MONEY!
...AND YOUR PLAN

It begins with your desire and plan. Your sales plan. Your game plan.
And your hard work plan.

Wait, you don't have one? Let me guess, you're soooo busy that you
don't have time to make one. You know what that means? It means
you're constantly on that hamster wheel reacting to anything and
anyone that comes your way. It means your actions are not intentional
or proactive, they're whack-a-mole at best. A sales plan contains
strategies, tactics, and goals that will prevent you from a slump and
help you get to winning streak.

It's human instinct to want to take care of the potential customer
who's called you - the instant gratification sale, rather than sit down
and make a plan. I'm not saying don't get the sale - get the sale, but
make time to make a plan.

Your TOTAL sales plan will empower you to hold yourself responsible
to daily/weekly/monthly goals and in turn make your number. Yes, I
just said empower and hold *yourself* responsible in the same sentence.
You didn't get in sales to be mediocre. You got in this to be a top
performer, so take the actions necessary to get there.

Your sales plan should contain what you need to do and by when (specific dates, goals and milestones) you need to complete to hit your sales targets.

Create your plan, implement, check your progress, track and tweak as needed and you'll be on your way to best in a New York Minute.

HERE'S WHAT TO DO:

Start with your "self-commitment" to work hard.
Go here *salesinanyminutebook.com/salesplan* and download my sales plan template.

DON'T TAKE ACTION UNTIL YOU HAVE WRITTEN DOWN WHAT YOU WANT THE ACTION TO ACHIEVE.

WHAT AMOUNT OF REVENUE DO YOU WANT TO BRING IN? SHOOT FOR THE MOON AND STARS, BUT MAKE SURE IT'S ACHIEVABLE AND REALISTIC. THEN FILL IN THE ACTIONS YOU NEED TO TAKE (AND BY WHEN) TO ACHIEVE YOUR ACCOMPLISHMENTS.

WHAT'S 15-30 MINUTES
OF YOUR TIME WORTH?

Many so-called experts say, "Don't give your time away for free. Don't give away your secrets, your value, your candy, your information or the prospect won't wanna work with you."

Let me tell you my secret: THAT'S BULLSHIT.

DO GIVE AWAY YOUR TIME, YOUR VALUE, YOUR INFORMATION AND SOME SECRETS. GIVE ENOUGH VALUE AND THE PROSPECT WILL FEEL COMPELLED TO WORK WITH YOU. MAKE THEM WANT MORE.

PERSONAL STORY:

I was introduced to Margaux Gunning, nutritionist extraordinaire, and she provided me with a free consultation call. I scheduled the call because I wanted help. Once we connected, I realized within the first 5 minutes that this health expert knew what she was talking about. She had AMAZING ideas and suggestions - stuff way beyond info I could Google. Pure VALUE. During the call, I determined that I would be doing myself a disservice by not hiring her.

Fifteen minutes turned into 30 as we talked about next steps and how we would work together. It's two years later and I am happy to call her a lifelong friend, her client for life, and hopefully her best referrer! Get Margaux's health strategies at *www.margauxgunning.com*.

THOSE 15 FREE MINUTES WORTH IT?

WHEN YOU GIVE YOUR HELP, YOUR IDEAS, AND YOUR STRATEGIES WITHOUT EXPECTATION, MORE TIMES THAN NOT, YOU'LL RECEIVE A SALE IN A NEW YORK MINUTE.

SALES IN A NY MINUTE
JENNIFER GLUCKOW

DOUBLE YOUR SALES
WITH ONE TECHNIQUE

It is more important to find out why people want to buy than it is to "sell." You can do that by asking potential buyers emotionally engaging questions instead of telling them boring things about you and your products or services.

Are you still selling by telling? Instead, try asking potential clients about themselves to get them interested in all things about you – and buying.

Do This:

Prepare questions that will get the conversation started with both comfort and truth. Make certain they're emotionally engaging, and about THEM. From simple questions like, "Where did you grow up?" or, "What was your path to achieving this position?" to business-oriented engagement questions like, "When I say (name of your product or service) what ONE word comes to mind?"

Get your prospects to reveal their motives by asking pre-prepared emotional questions. Uncover your path to the sale by changing from TELL to ASK and your sales will double in a New York Minute.

SALES IN A NY MINUTE
JENNIFER GLUCKOW

THE BEST ~~WAY~~ WHY TO MAKE A SALE

Finding the "needs" of a prospect is thought of as the most important part of the sale - not quite true. You must also discover WHY they need it. Finding out your prospect's real "why" is the most important part of the selling process. Why he or she needs it is more important than the need itself.

The biggest mistake salespeople make is trying to sell for the wrong reasons - their own reasons. Customers don't care what you do, or what you're selling, or why you're selling it, unless they perceive they need it AND it helps them.

PEOPLE DON'T BUY FOR YOUR REASONS — THEY BUY — FOR THEIR REASONS.

— JEFFREY GITOMER

DO THIS:

Position your presentation and your solutions around their needs and you'll get them to buy in a New York Minute.

SALES IN A NY MINUTE
JENNIFER GLUCKOW

YOUR CUSTOMER'S "WHY" IS THREE FEET DEEP

The real "why" you're after (why the customer wants to buy) may be 3 or 4 "why questions" deep. When you get a superficial why answer, ask why again. It will get you closer to the real truth.

For example, the prospect says,

- I want to increase our productivity. Ask, "Why?"
- Costs are increasing and we need more profit. Ask, "Why?"
- Well, we're having to reduce the workforce, and we need a machine that will help the administrative person bear the extra tasks she'll be taking on. AHA! - the real "why."

GRAB YOUR IMPLE-MENTOR

Go at least three feet deep to find out why they buy and the sale will be yours in a New York Minute.

"

SALESPEOPLE ARE TOO BUSY TRYING TO FIGURE OUT "HOW" AND OVERLOOK THE REAL SECRET TO SELLING, THE CUSTOMER'S "WHY."

JENNIFER GLUCKOW
@JENINANYMINUTE

WHEN THE CUSTOMER'S

URGENCY TO BUY

·············· IS HIGH, ··············

THEIR SENSITIVITY

TO PRICE

IS LOW

JENNIFER GLUCKOW
@JENINANYMINUTE

TWO WAYS TO THE TOP

There are two ways to go to the top of the Empire State Building:
One is go to the back of the line, the other is go to the front of the line.

Where would you rather be? The answer is, what price are you willing to pay to get to the top of the Empire State Building? Some people are willing to pay more to not stand in line, so they invented, "run to the front of the line, pay double, and be next." At first it seems outrageous until the line is 500 people deep, and your urgency to buy has greater value than your desire to wait in line. At some point, price is no longer a consideration.

Many of your customers have the same urgency, you just don't know which ones. Your job is not just to make a sale. Your job is to understand your customer well enough to know when they're willing to run to the front of the line.

TAKE ACTION:

Most salespeople whine about price or price being too high (or the line being too long) and have no understanding that some people are willing to pay double to get what they want right now. Uncover your customer's urgency to buy so that you too can make even more profitable sales in a New York Minute.

❝

BE THE HELPER AND THE HELP YOUR CUSTOMERS ARE HOPING FOR.

SALES IN A NY MINUTE

JENNIFER GLUCKOW

ARE YOU HELPING
OR SELLING?

I worked at a company that had salespeople and Account Managers. The Account Managers would sit with the customer a couple times per year to review their account, figure out what was going right, what could be improved and how we could help.

Sounds great, but it was a major problem. The salesperson didn't attend. The Account Managers would become the trusted advisor, the helper, and the salesperson would lose credibility because they only showed up when it was time to renew or upsell the account.

When do you show up? Do you show up only when it's time to collect a check? The Account Managers were able to recommend products or services based on the trust they built through HELPING.

HERE'S THE LESSON:

Be the helper and the help all times of the year. Look out for your customer's concerns and problems. Check in on their account and make sure they are continuously better off with your solution.

Maintain your relationship every day, not just on a sales day and you'll be helping more customers (and making more sales) in a New York Minute.

HELP DON'T SELL

Too many salespeople take a hard (non-emotional) approach to selling. No one wants to be sold and no one wants to feel like they're being sold.

Think about it, do you?

As humans, we want and need help and we want valuable information.

The best salespeople help. The best salespeople educate, inform, inspire, and give their customers tools to help them grow their business, win more sales, and gain more profit.

Ask Yourself: Are you selling at your "helping" best?

Helping begins with your desire and your actions. Are you always coming from a desire to help or are you blinded by the sale?

DO THIS:

Make it your desire to help, not sell, and soon your customer will be helping you with more sales in a New York Minute.

SALES IN A NY MINUTE
JENNIFER GLUCKOW

SHOW DON'T TELL

Nobody wants you to spew information about you, your company, your products and services that they could have found on Google.

Prospects want to be shown, in an engaging, friendly and fun manner, how you can help them grow more, profit more, and win more.

Think about Instagram. Instagram has a billion users. And it's the social media platform with the most engagement. People are most engaged in a platform with the least words. Their icon is a camera, not a script. You go on Instagram to see visuals, not read the captions. But, if the picture is interesting and engaging, then you may want to learn more and read the caption.

The same is true with a prospect. If what you show is engaging, then the prospect may want to learn more. And people will buy.

Are you selling by showing or selling by telling?

YOUR CHALLENGE:

Use images, videos, stories and testimonials or voice of customer to demonstrate how you can help.

Show don't tell and your customer will have top engagement in a New York Minute.

"

HELP DON'T SELL.
SHOW DON'T TELL.
PROVE LIKE HELL!

JENNIFER GLUCKOW
@JENINANYMINUTE

PROVE LIKE HELL - WITH A CUSTOMER (AKA: STOP BRAGGING)

You can tell your prospect how great you are, but you talking about how great you are is not as believable as your customer talking about how great you are. People want truth and the best way to get it is PROOF.

THE BEST FORM OF PROOF IS A VIDEO TESTIMONIAL.
THE SECOND BEST FORM IS A WRITTEN TESTIMONIAL.
THE WORST FORM OF PROOF IS YOU AND YOUR SLIDE DECK.

MAKE IT HAPPEN:

Earn proof-positive customer testimonials with quality products and amazing service, then feature your customers on your website, your sales meetings, and your social media.

When people see others talking about how great it is to work with you, they will be more inclined to buy from you, and pay your price in a New York Minute.

EXTRA! MINUTE

Go to *salesinanyminutebook.com* and you will find more!

SELLING · WINNING STRATEGIES

DETAILS TO SALES TO DETAILS

On roadtrips, my parents would challenge me to find hidden objects. They would name the object and I would try to find it. This trained me, from a very young age, to both seek and observe the smallest details.

On a sales call, noticing hard-to-find details can often be the most important clue to getting an order. Your order. What do you look at when you're on a sales call? Are you so busy "pitching and showing slides" that you forget to look around? Look around, and modify your presentation accordingly! Don't just look for trophies and family photos. Look at and listen to your client's non-verbal cues – observe their gestures. Listen to their questions, and interpret their subtle messages. Determine their real concerns.

TAKE ACTION:

Take notes in your sales meeting. Write your observations. Know their sports teams, special celebratory dates and what motives will make them buy. Review your notes before your next visit and use them to deepen your relationship and get the sale.

Once you uncover the details underneath the big picture, you'll be observing your way to more sales in a New York Minute.

"COMMON GROUND
LOWERS BARRIERS
[TO SALES]
AND RAISES PENS

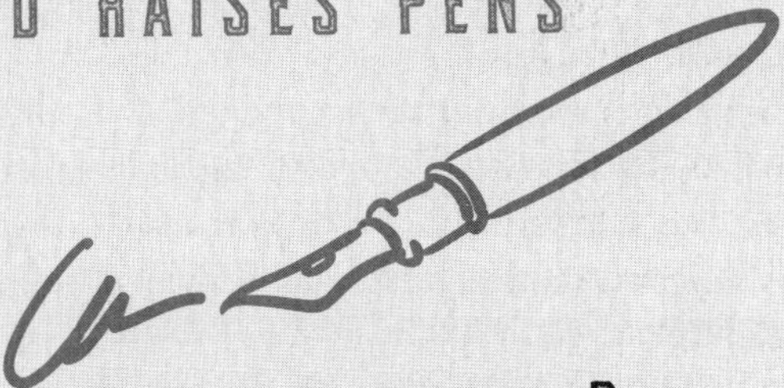

[TO SIGN ORDERS]."

JENNIFER GLUCKOW
@JENINANYMINUTE

NOT GETTING PAST THE GATEKEEPER?

Here's why: You couldn't engage. You were salesy or not friendly or both. You made the mistake of being aggressive or pushy, or thinking they cared about you.

Here's what: Figure out what they care about or need. Do they have remarkable things on their desk? Art? Knickknacks? Family photos? Have you prepared for them? Ask sincere questions and show genuine interest. Build mild rapport. Then, give the gatekeeper a good reason to let you meet their boss. A good reason is *not* "so you can sell them your stuff or save them money." That's *your* reason, and they don't care about *you* or *your* reason. A good reason is something about profit, productivity, or morale. Build a solid smile exchange, offer value, and you'll get past the gatekeeper in a New York Minute.

GRAB YOUR IMPLE-MENTOR

Make a list of the top 5 gatekeepers in your life. Next to each gatekeeper, make notes about them - rapport-building notes. Write about why they should let you through. Knowing your why will help you articulate it better when it comes time for your ask. Put your plan into action and refine it for 30 days.

"SALES IS NOT A

manipulative battle,

IT'S A CONVERSATION,
A VALUE-BASED OFFER,
AND A RELATIONSHIP."

JENNIFER GLUCKOW
@JENINANYMINUTE

CONSISTENCY IN SALES

I went to South Carolina on a self-imposed writing retreat.

While most of my day was spent writing, I took the time away to get back to my favorite sport...tennis.

Having played well over 10,000 hours, just none in the past 4 years, I had been hesitant to get back on the court. If you're as competitive as I am, you don't want to lose and look lousy doing it! If you're in sales, you probably know the feeling.

My first day back to the game was like old times.

IT WAS A MIX BETWEEN HITTING THE PERFECT SHOT AND MISSING AN EASY SHOT.

But I realized that I still have it – muscle memory kicked in and I was swinging backhands and forehands like no time had passed.

Well, some time had passed since I had last played. It was clear to me that time off had affected my timing. I had some great shots, but they weren't consistently great.

TO BE CONSISTENTLY GREAT:

- Practice daily
- Keep your eye on the sale
- Know when to swing
- Don't jump over the net until the customer pays

HOW'S YOUR TIMING?

Make sure you're meeting with your prospects when they are ready to buy. If you get there too late, you'll miss your best shot.

HERE'S THE CONSISTENCY KEY:

Keep your eye on the ball - and on the ballpoint pen, and keep your eye on the sale.

THE KEY TO WINNING IS BEING READY EVERY TIME. CONSISTENCY PLAYS GREAT AND PAYS GREAT. GIVE IT YOUR BEST SHOT EVERY TIME AND YOU'LL BE MAKING MORE SALES IN A NEW YORK MINUTE.

JENNIFER GLUCKOW
@JENINANYMINUTE

x

SELLING · WINNING STRATEGIES

CONTROL. CONSISTENCY. CONFIDENCE.

As I was playing tennis and thinking about my New York Minutes, my tennis instructor, Tory Painter, hit me right in the brain. She said, "Winning is all about control, consistency and confidence. And it's all about staying positive." Balls were flying by me at 80 miles per hour, and whoosh - she served a stroke of genius! Winning a tennis match is like winning the sale. Tennis anyone?

Winning the tennis match: Great shots need to be consistently great if you want to win. Consistency comes from practice. Your consistency will build confidence, and confidence will build more consistency and control. It's a combo cycle. And it's a winning cycle.

Winning the Sale: Whether you play tennis or not, it doesn't matter (unless you want to hit with me on the courts). Here's how the control, consistency, confidence cycle, the win cycle, relates to sales:

- **Control.** Just like in tennis, your preparation and follow-through determine your control. Command control of the sale by doing the majority of the work ahead of time - prepare for the sale so you can command control of the sale. Prepare questions that guide the conversation towards the sale. It's not just about controlling the ball, it's about controlling yourself and your enthusiasm to play and win.

- **Consistency.** The key to winning is being great EVERY time. Consistency plays great and pays great. How consistently great are you? Practice leads to consistency. There's no shortcut. Practice makes you better. Study yourself. Film your sales conversations and watch yourself - learn from your good shots, er sales, and learn from your not-so-good ones. When you practice the foundational skills and become an expert, your muscle memory and your sales memory will kick in at exactly the right time. Your consistency will create more opportunities to increase your win ratio. Consistency is not just about playing the game, it's about having the right attitude, the right beliefs, and the right mindset before you even begin.
- **Confidence.** As you become more consistent and win more sales, your self-confidence grows. When your self-confidence grows, your positive self-talk thrives and you gain even more control for the next sale. The confidence of a win propels you to win again.

GRAB YOUR IMPLE-MENTOR
Take the quiz.

Believe you will win. Control your sale with best-preparation. Create a consistency checklist. Practice your pitch, your questions, your rapport building. Practice by doing. Make a list of past wins and think about how you were in control during those sales. Increase your confidence and increase your sales.

Keep your eye on the ball and your eye on the sale, and with consistency, control, and confidence, you'll be making more sales in a New York Minute.

SALES IN A NY MINUTE
JENNIFER GLUCKOW

BIGGEST SALES EXCUSES

Salespeople try to justify why they aren't making quotas by blaming everything and everyone, rather than just stepping up to the challenge, and taking responsibility for poor performance.

Here are the 3 biggest excuses:

1. No one is buying right now. Well, guess what buddy? People are buying, they're just not buying from you.
2. The price is too high.
3. The product sucks.

Those are bullshit excuses. Don't let challenges turn into excuses. And don't let excuses get in the way of *your* success. Document your challenges, take responsibility to create value-based answers for those challenges, and implement a NO EXCUSE policy.

THINK ABOUT THIS:

How much more do you think you could you grow if you weren't allowed to make excuses? What would your new results be?

Answering these questions and putting them into practice will take time, but the reward is making more sales in a New York Minute.

SALES IN A NY MINUTE
JENNIFER GLUCKOW

POSTPONING VS. PROCRASTINATION

You know what procrastination is – come on, you do it all the time – but very few understand postponing.

Here's the secret: Not postponing is a key element in sales success – postponing challenges the depth of your commitment. Not just commitment to your company or to your clients, your commitment to yourself.

Picture This: There was a blizzard, and you had a sales appointment scheduled on the other side of town. The roads are barely passable but not impossible. Your client is warm and cozy, sipping hot chocolate, waiting for your arrival. Would you show up or stay in? Would you postpone the meeting for a "better day" or do whatever it takes to get there? Blame the snow or brave the frozen tundra?

Dude, you go no matter what! Show the customer you're committed and reliable, and when you get there, celebrate the weather – and the fact that your competition postponed their meeting.

TAKE ACTION:

It's not just about making the meeting, it's a display of your character and fortitude. Don't postpone. Make the meeting and you'll be making the sale and sipping hot chocolate in a New York Minute.

FINDING THE PAIN

Finding the pain in your customer is meaningless if you have your own pain, because all you do is focus on your own pain. And, even if you're trying to stay positive, any sort of pain can get in your way.

Last year I went on a sales call (Luckily for me, I think they were sold before we met), and I had the biggest headache of my life. By the time I left, it had turned into a migraine. I have no idea how I performed because I was working 10 times as hard just to act as if nothing was bothering me. I didn't want to let my physical pain get in the way of their sales pain.

GRAB YOUR IMPLE-MENTOR
Ask yourself:

- How's your health? How's your sales health?
- How does your health affect your attitude and your performance?
- What is holding you back from full sales achievements?

Clear your pains and be 100% focused on your customer pains, and their gains (and yours) will come your way in a New York Minute.

THE "TAKE ADVANTAGE" SALE

Here's a secret: you don't need to sell alone. Ask your boss to join you on sales meetings. Some salespeople are scared to present in front of their boss. Update: Your boss will know when you're making a mistake, but the customer won't. **Do this:** Prepare 3 times more than you would normally prepare and you won't be nervous.

REALITY: YOUR BOSS WILL HELP YOU CLOSE THE SALE.

When it's time for feedback, have an open mind. There's nothing worse than asking for feedback and then getting defensive or trying to dispute the feedback. If you want to improve, stay silent and listen with an open mind to your boss's suggestions then act on their suggestions. And, the next time you make a sales call, call your boss afterward to let him/her know what you are now doing differently.

Note: You don't have to ask for "feedback." Your boss will proactively provide it.

DO THIS:

When you're going on a sales call with your boss, prepare, listen, take action and follow through, and you, and your sales, will be improving in a New York Minute.

SALES IN A NY MINUTE

JENNIFER GLUCKOW

ARE YOU THE CEO OF YOUR TERRITORY AND YOUR LIFE?

Top-performing salespeople act differently than other reps.
The biggest difference is self-imposed leadership.

Top performers are not just salespeople, they are leaders. They take responsibility for their actions, and they own their quota as if they're managing numbers for their own business. Those reps are the CEO of their territory.

Think about your role as a CEO. A CEO must take full responsibility for wins and losses, they're responsible for making the numbers, and they must lead others to action. They need to create reputable, value-provided relationships. The same goes for YOU, a top-performing salesperson.

PERSONAL EXPERIENCE:

Lucy was one of my top performers. When she was given a quota, she would call me and tell me how she would get there, not wait for me to ask her to come up with a plan. Right after getting a new quota, she announced her pregnancy and made sure to tell me in the same conversation that she was going to meet, no beat, her quota. And, she proceeded to tell me how she would beat it - exactly what she needed to do and by when to crush her quota 3 months early. Here's the best part - she followed her plan and crushed her quota, 3 months earlier than everyone else! She CEO'd her departure and is now a CEO mother.

DO THIS:

Rate yourself on your leadership actions. How often do you lead others? Are you the CEO for your territory and your life? How often do you plan strategically and follow your plan? How often are you planning for success, not just quota? Write down what it will take to get to the next leadership level. Then take CEO action.

Make a CEO plan. Follow it. And you'll be crushing your numbers in a New York Minute.

66

TOP PERFORMERS
ARE NOT JUST SALESPEOPLE.
THEY ARE LEADERS.

JENNIFER GLUCKOQW
@JENINANYMINUTE

117

"YOUR PRICE IS TOO LOW"

Wouldn't that be nice to hear?! How your customer values your offering and price depends on how you've positioned it. Did you show up and throw up or did you listen to their needs and discover why they want to buy? Did you offer REAL value?

If a customer values your offering enough, they may be willing to buy it at almost any price. Think about a nice piece of art – you might be willing to pay $100 for a reprint, while someone else may be willing to pay $100,000 for the original. It all depends on perceived value. The price that they pay is based on *their* perceived benefit.

HERE'S THE LESSON:

What's your customer's perceived value and perceived benefit? Find out what they value and you may hear that your price is too low in a New York Minute.

PRICE VS. BULLSHIT (THE MYTH OF PRICE-BASED DECISIONS BUSTED)

"Your price is too high." Ever hear that objection? The salespeople who believe the customer actually can't afford it, are still waiting for Santa Claus to answer their letter.

The reality of this objection is, the customer doesn't perceive your value to be worth your asking price. But I wonder if you believe the same thing? First, YOU must believe that your product or service is worth more than the price. If you don't, why should others believe it?

Next, help the buyer understand your value by asking them questions and finding out what matters to them most. It doesn't matter what you care about. Figure out what matters to them. Why do they want to buy? Uncover their real reason for buying and you'll go from bullshit to buying in a New York Minute.

TAKE ACTION:

"Price" is the most often heard objection. To overcome it, you must be fully prepared. Make a list of questions that you can use to uncover what matters to your buyer. Use those questions on your next sales call and write down any additional questions you end up asking. After the sales meeting, refine your list so that as you visit customers, you're able to ask better "why-discovery" questions each time.

"THE **WINNER** IS MORE LIKELY THE PERSON **WHO FOLLOWS THROUGH.** WAY MORE LIKELY THAN THE PERSON WHO JUST FOLLOWS UP."

JENNIFER GLUCKOW
@JENINANYMINUTE

SALES IN A NY MINUTE
JENNIFER GLUCKOW

FOLLOWING THROUGH
INSTEAD OF FOLLOWING UP

Professional slot machine players know how many times they need to put money in the machine to hit a jackpot. They know if they walk away too soon, someone will come by, put one coin in the machine and win the jackpot. They could have played for hours and invested a ton of money, but walking away too soon means they could lose everything.

Salespeople love jackpots, but don't always have the consistent follow-through - *not* follow up - that it takes to get the jackpot. Just like the person who puts ONE coin into a slot machine, and expects a jackpot, a salesperson often expects to follow up once, twice, maybe three times and have a better chance to get the sale.

The winner is most likely the person who follows *through* - not a guaranteed win, but more likely than the person who just follows up.

HERE'S THE DIFFERENCE:

Follow-up is checking in and asking for the sale. Follow-through is staying in touch with value messages and being assertively relentless until you get the sale, or are told you lost it.

Persistent and consistent follow through leads to more sales in a New York Minute.

SALES IN A NY MINUTE
JENNIFER GLUCKOW

SAME TIME NEXT WEEK

Ever follow up with a prospect and leave a message, hoping for a call back? But then not get one? So, you call and you call, you email, you call, you email, you call, but no one gets back to you? It's frustrating! It's maddening! Oh, and it's also preventable.

HERE'S THE SECRET:

IF I DON'T MAKE THE SALE, I NEVER END A PHONE CALL WITHOUT A FIRM FOLLOW-UP APPOINTMENT.

HERE'S THE STRATEGY:

Say to your prospect, "Let's reconnect the same time next week! How does that work for you?" Note: Don't ask IF they can reconnect. Ask if the time you're choosing is okay – your question will assume that you're going to reconnect. If they don't want to schedule a follow-up, then you probably don't have the sale. If you can find out why and if it's saveable, you'll save time and get to the truth in a New York Minute.

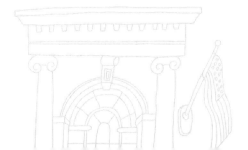

SALES IN A NY MINUTE

JENNIFER GLUCKOW

USE SELFIES TO INCREASE SALES

Your meeting is going great, but you don't think you're going to make the sale. You'll need to follow-up. Ask to take a selfie. Take a photo with your prospect or take a photo of something remarkable that's all about them. And then, send them an amazing follow-up email and thank you note that includes the photo. Remind them about your next meeting that I am certain you scheduled before you left. This will help your follow-up in a New York Minute.

NOTE: SELFIE VS. SELFISH

- **Post for others.** To help them or inspire them. Don't post a selfie with your customer if it's just serving yourself.
- **Praise others.** You will gain more respect by showing off something THEY do well, than trying to talk about something YOU do well.
- **Promote others.** The law of reciprocity is there, trust it, believe in it, just don't expect it.

TAKE ACTION:

Got the shot? Great! Now email it to your client with a meeting recap and next steps. Or better yet, text it to them if you built a good enough relationship to get their cell phone number. If you didn't get the shot with your client, take a selfie outside their office and let them know you're looking forward to your return meeting. Just remember: they'd much rather see a shot with themselves in it than just you!

SALES IN A NY MINUTE

JENNIFER GLUCKOW

DO YOU GIVE UP TOO SOON?

Do you give up easily? Take the first no? In 1953 the late, great, Elmer Leterman wrote a book called, *The Sale Begins When the Customer Says NO* – and that mantra is still true more than 60 years later.

More often than not, the answer is not "yes" on the first sales call. Your job is to call on your positive attitude and your positive persistence. Set an appointment for the next step in the sale, document the sales cycle status, and get ready for the next step. Find reasons to stay in touch with value messages. The object in sales and selling is to NOT give up. Instead, convert those feelings and thoughts to how you WILL make the sale.

MAKE IT COUNT:

Be more inspired, be more positive, be more resilient, be more informed, be more prepared and you'll convert no to yes, in a New York Minute.

SALES IN A NY MINUTE
JENNIFER GLUCKOW

SALES
PERSISTENCE

I'm sure you've heard, "no" or "not right now" or "let me think about it" or "I'll get back to you." Did you quit? The difference between winning and losing is persistence. Napoleon Hill, Author of *Think and Grow Rich*, said, "Patience, persistence and perspiration make an unbeatable combination for success."

In NYC, patience is almost non-existent, but in sales, you have to have patience to survive. Patience with yourself, your sales process, your follow-up, your follow-through and especially with your customer.

Persistence is learned at age 4 when you learned to ride a bike. What did it feel like each time you fell? Get back up each time? You persisted through humiliation, scraped knees and maybe a few tears. Through patience and persistence sometimes you sweat a little. The good news is: perspiration never hurt anyone, sweat for the sale.

DO THIS:

Get back on your bike, get back in your car, get back to your computer, and get back on the phone and exercise your patience, your persistence and your perspiration and you'll be a winning and in-shape salesperson in a New York Minute.

SALES IN A NY MINUTE
JENNIFER GLUCKOW

IN SELLING, "NO" MEANS "NOT RIGHT NOW"

How do you react, respond and recover from a NO? Do you carry that negative mindset into your next sale and let it affect your potential next yes? I'm not just talking about a "no" in sales, but think about what you do when you get a "no" in life.

In high school, I wanted to get a job. The first company I applied to in NYC turned me down - they thought I was too young. Rather than fret about it, or become sad, or wallow in my rejection, I said, "no problem!" I went to their competition in New Jersey, applied there, got the job, and became one of the top reps. Too young? Nope, just too young for them.

YOUR ACTION:

DON'T GIVE UP,
PRACTICE YOUR PERSISTENCE &
YOUR RESILIENCE

AND YOU'LL BE GETTING

YOUR WAY IN A

MINUTE

JENNIFER GLUCKOW
@JENINANYMINUTE

SALES IN A NY MINUTE
JENNIFER GLUCKOW

PEOPLE WHO
CANCEL/DON'T SHOW

You made the appointment. Tuesday at 3 o'clock. You're so happy, you can't stand it.

You prepare, you get excited, you hop on zoom.us at 2:59, and by 3:11 it becomes apparent that something has gone drastically wrong – your client has stiffed you. You don't wanna swear – you're thinking, "I have to be positive!" But all the time you're really thinking, "that !*!#?! no-show!"

Or you make an appointment for 3 o'clock on Tuesday and at 2 o'clock you get a phone call or an email and the prospect says, "Something has come up" and while you thought it was a great appointment, he says he'll call you next week to reschedule. **Rats!**

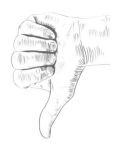

HERE'S WHAT TO DO:

First of all, go take a cold shower because it's part of sales. If you're not willing to accept that part of the selling process, then get a job at McDonald's where sales are much easier. Or begin a confirmation process that makes showing or not cancelling more likely.

Send calendar invites, emails with a positive slant, and text if you can. Offer a great reason for them to want to show – give them something of value – advice, a relevant article – a link – something that shows you are going to become a value provider (not just their salesperson), in advance of the meeting.

AND BE PREPARED SO THAT IF THE PROSPECT DOES SHOW, YOU'RE 100% READY. MORE THAN HALF OF YOUR NO-SHOWS OR CANCELLATIONS CAN BE AVOIDED WITH YOUR SELLING PROCESS.

AND YOU'LL HAVE MORE PEOPLE SHOW UP IN A NEW YORK MINUTE.

SALES IN A NY MINUTE
JENNIFER GLUCKOW

SELLING OR DROWNING?

If someone threw you into the deep end of the pool, and you could not swim, what would you do?

The answer is: you would rely on your adrenaline and your instincts. Your adrenaline would kick in giving you that extra strength and save yourself from drowning.

You would fight to live or win or swim or get out of the pool. And you would fight like hell.

REALITY CHECK:

When you saved yourself and got out of the pool, would you be angry or triumphant?

Because if you would be angry, you wouldn't come up with anything creative to say or do. You could either wear saving yourself as a badge of honor or hold on to anger against the idiot that threw you in...

Over time, when things don't go your way, one of two things can happen:

1. You can become helpless and complain, become cynical, and drown. OR
2. You can say to yourself, "That will never happen again," and learn what you need to do to prevent it from re-occurring.

HERE'S THE SALES EXAMPLE:

YOUR CUSTOMER SAYS, "NO." DO YOU FIGHT LIKE HELL OR GIVE UP? DO YOU SINK OR SWIM? WHAT'S YOUR NATURAL INSTINCT?

While there is no badge of honor in sales, my recommendation is that you break down and invest in sales lessons so that you can float to the top in your next sales meeting and turn panic into profit - no's into yeses - in a New York Minute.

SALES IN A NY MINUTE
JENNIFER GLUCKOW

NEED FAST ANSWERS?
JUST GOOGLE IT.

How often do you try to figure out answers on your own? Self-teach concepts that could help further your sales?

When I was younger, I was with my sister (who is 10 years younger than I am) and I told her, "I'm gonna call mom to ask her how to cook the chicken." She said, "Why? You could just Google that." And she was right. NOTE: she said this in 1999, a year after Google was founded!

How many times has someone asked you something and you've thought, "I don't know! Just Google it!" If this hasn't happened, that means your first instinct is not to Google it.

Google is a learned science. When you Google for an answer, make sure you're finding legit sources. Legit information. This takes both practice and patience. The depth of Google is un-ending. Google is a valuable sales resource. Companies, customers, prospects, even boyfriends, use Google. Learn to master it, not just Google it.

DO THIS:

Make Google your first resource, master it, and you'll be answering your own questions (and others' questions) in a New York Minute.

GOOGLE NOW PROCESSES
OVER 40,000 SEARCH QUERIES
EVERY SECOND, WHICH TRANSLATES
TO OVER 3.5 BILLION SEARCHES
PER DAY AND 1.2 TRILLION SEARCHES
PER YEAR WORLDWIDE.

GO AHEAD AND GOOGLE "HOW MANY TIMES A DAY
DO PEOPLE USE GOOGLE?"

YOU'LL FIND THAT ANSWER!

THEN GOOGLE YOURSELF.
IT'S AN ANSWER YOU MAY NOT LIKE.

SALES IN A NY MINUTE
JENNIFER GLUCKOW

HAVE YOU EARNED THE CLOSE?

You earn the right to close the sale from the minute you start communicating with the prospect.

Ask yourself:

- Did you show up on time? Were you prepared to win?
- Build a solid rapport?
- Demonstrate how they win? Prove value?
- Are you speaking with the right person - the one who can actually say, "Yes"?

HERE'S THE LESSON:

Although the close is the last part of the sale, your closing rate is determined by your actions throughout the entire sale. Start earning the sale from the very beginning and you'll be closing more sales in a New York Minute.

"

YOU EARN THE RIGHT
TO CLOSE THE SALE
FROM THE MINUTE
YOU START THE SALE.

JENNIFER GLUCKOW
@JENINANYMINUTE

"

Assume
THE SALE

IS YOURS.

JENNIFER GLUCKOW
@JENINANYMINUTE

SALES IN A NY MINUTE
JENNIFER GLUCKOW

THE SALE IS MINE

I assume the sale is mine and you should assume the sale is yours from the very first minute you meet with a prospect. You can do that by treating every prospect like they're your best customer.

Ask questions along the way that confirm your assumption like:

"How do you see this fitting in with your team?"
"How do you see yourself using this solution?"
"How will this solution impact the way you do business?"

Ask assumptive closing questions like:

"When would you like to get started?"
"Which option are you going with?"
"When would you like it installed?"

Many times you may already know the answer, but you should ask so that the customer has an opportunity to visualize how they will use whatever you're selling and communicate the value that's most important to them.

HERE'S THE REAL SECRET:

Your belief and assumptive mindset will tip the sale in your direction from the first New York Minute to the close.

FANCY SCHMANCY
CLOSING THE SALE TECHNIQUE

Google "how to close a sale" and you'll get all kinds of strategies and techniques.

Here's a secret: You don't need a fancy schmancy "closing technique."
Think about it: Do you want to be closed?

DO THIS INSTEAD:

Throughout the entire sales process, be real, genuine and authentic. Be confident of the value you offer, understand how your product or service is going to impact (and help) your customer. Communicate that value to your prospect in terms of how they win. Communicate customer success stories, or better yet, bring videos with customer success stories so that your prospect can hear directly from your current customers.

Don't just say it, prove it. If the prospect likes you and believes in you and believes that your products and services will help them win, they'll buy. No "CLOSE" needed. Be their consultant, their trusted advisor, their profit producer, their time saver, their problem solver and you'll be closing more sales - without closing - in a New York Minute.

MAMA SAYS, IF YOU DON'T ASK YOU DON'T GET

Growing up, my mom used to preach, "Jennifer, if you don't ask, you don't get." And she preached this to me all the time. I'm sure your mom has preached to you as well.

I got the message at age 12, just in time for the holidays. Of course, my holiday list doubled that year – I'm sure my parents loved that! But in sales, many people are afraid to ask – they're afraid to ask simple rapport-building questions up to and including, asking for the sale.

SO I CHALLENGE YOU:

Do you ask? Successful salespeople ask the right questions. Emotionally engaging questions. Questions that help find common ground and build rapport. Questions that uncover needs and motives for purchase. And of course, they ask for the sale.

I wonder if you ask for the sale. Or do you assume the sale when they ask for a proposal? Why don't you just do what I do? Take my mother's advice and ask. No matter what kind of sales call I'm in, I ask for the sale every time.

My mom has led me to sales. And I promise, if you take my mom's advice, she will lead you to more sales in a New York Minute.

"

AFTER YOU CLOSE THE SALE,
CREATE A DOMINO CLOSE EFFECT
by going after more
SALES RIGHT AWAY.

JENNIFER GLUCKOW
@JENINANYMINUTE

SALES IN A NY MINUTE
JENNIFER GLUCKOW

WIN THE NEXT SALE

What do you do right *after* you close a sale? Let's be real, if you're like most salespeople, you count your commision.

What *should* you be doing after you close a sale? Instead of counting your commissions, go make another sale!

Think about it. Right after you close a sale, your emotions are high. They're at their peak. You're excited, you're confident, you're ready. This is the BEST time to go out and close another deal.

HERE'S THE LESSON:

Create a domino close effect by going after more sales right away.

Want to create a major chain reaction? Pack your Mondays with sales meetings with decision-makers who can say yes. Start the week off with a sale, and you'll be closing more and more deals in a New York Minute.

#MAKEASALEMONDAY

REJECTION IS AN 8X OPPORTUNITY

You just got rejected.

Did you take it personally? Will you give up? Are you over sales? Reject that!

HERE'S HOW TO TURN THE POWER OF REJECTION INTO AN 8X OPPORTUNITY.

- **Education opportunity.** Learn why you lost. Learn how you can improve. The feeling of rejection will last for a few minutes. The lessons learned will last a lifetime.
- **Celebration opportunity.** Throw a "no!" celebration. You should be jumping up and down saying, "YES I got another No!" Celebrate the fact that you're one step closer to a yes!
- **Energy opportunity.** Use that energy, your fight or flight response, in a positive way. Turn that Mmmmmph into inspiration to get more creative on your next sale.
- **Attitude opportunity.** You have a choice - harbor the negative emotion from your rejection or make it positive. Your choice, your opportunity.
- **Relationship opportunity.** Now that your prospect does not want to move forward, you can build an even stronger relationship

when they see you still want one. This is not a transaction opportunity. This is a long-term relationship opportunity.

- **Resilience opportunity.** Your internal strength. Your internal ability to react, respond and recover. You got this!
- **Silver lining opportunity.** I am in ever-search of the rainbow at the end of a rainstorm. You may not find it right away, but when you do, you'll be grateful you got rejected. Know there is always a silver lining.
- **Sales opportunity.** So, you lost one! N.O. = **Next One**! Go get the next sale.

When you turn your rejections into opportunities, you'll be creating more and more and more opportunity in a New York Minute.

"THE FEELING OF REJECTION WILL LAST FOR A FEW MINUTES. THE LESSONS LEARNED WILL LAST A LIFETIME."

JENNIFER GLUCKOW
@JENINANYMINUTE

"NO" MEANS THE "NEXT ONE" COULD BE A YES!

When was the last time you were rejected? I'm not asking you to think back to high school or the dating scene. Think about the biggest rejections in your career. Turned down for a promotion? Turned down for a job? Turned down for a sale?

What did you do when you got rejected? Get upset? Get mad? Blame others? Did that negative energy help you or hurt your next sale. When you get a sales rejection, you gotta shake it off. You gotta let it empower you to go find a yes. I look at NO as an acronym for Next One. When someone tells me no, I get excited knowing that I can move on to the Next One and make the sale with them. You should do the same.

HERE'S THE LESSON:

Go from "no" to next one's a "yes" with the right outlook in a New York Minute.

Here's what to do: Stay positive. Learn from the last no. Figure out what you can do better with the next prospect and go get the sale.

SALES IN A NY MINUTE
JENNIFER GLUCKOW

THANK YOU,
NEXT!

I have friends struggling to "make it" as an actor or performer on Broadway. Their "job" is basically: studying, practicing, preparing, trying out for different roles, and accepting rejection most of the time.

But the main part of their job is performing. Performing at a superior level to all of the other would-be actors and performers. To be successful, actors must have an ability to prepare, persevere, and perform... all through being told, "we'll call you," or "thank you, next!" Successful actors, like successful salespeople, don't blame others; they just check their attitude, rededicate themselves to winning, practice more, and move on to the next audition – or in your case, the next appointment. Do you take rejection as a challenge to improve?

Every time you get rejected, think about how you could have done better, while nurturing the contacts you've made for a possibility in the future.

TAKE ACTION:

Don't give up! Get up, get happy, and learn from the lesson. Keep trying out for the part of "vendor of choice." Do that, and you'll pass the audition – the sales audition, and your name will go up in lights on Broadway in a New York Minute.

KICK THE SALES SLUMP

Wanna get out of a sales slump?

First realize there is no silver bullet.
YOU are the only person who can dig yourself outta that hole.
YOU are the only person who can take yourself from sales slump to over the hump – and realize you're not gonna get out of there immediately. BUT, you will get there one sale at a time.

Here are a few strategies you should implement if you find yourself in a rut. One or two or more may help you now and in the future...

CHECK YOURSELF

Record yourself. Listen to your phone calls and presentations. They are more than eye opening, and they will likely make you laugh or cringe. BUT you will learn from them. Make a list of what to do more of and what not to do ever again. Read that list before every appointment for the next month until it becomes a habit.

COFFEE CALENDAR

Add some customers to your coffee. Call your best customers and make appointments for coffee EVERY MORNING for the next 30 days. Ask them why they bought. Talk small talk at first, then ask them what they like about working with you. Reinforce your beliefs through theirs.

KEEP SWINGING

Keep swinging, er, selling. The great Hank Aaron said, "My motto was always to keep swinging. Whether I was in a slump or feeling badly or having trouble off the field, the only thing to do was keep swinging." Keep calling, keep prospecting, keep meeting with clients, keep pitching, keep trying. Keep swinging.

When your sales are slow and you feel like you're in a slump, it's easy to slow down or stop... Stop meeting with prospects, stop prospecting, stop putting yourself in a winning situation.

SOUNDS LIKE A SELF-FULFILLING PROPHECY. EH?

TAKE ACTION:

Why don't you start taking the right actions, double your output, and double your lead generation efforts. Prepare for sales calls with an extra hard swing, and you'll be going, going, GONE! in a New York Minute.

TAKE A WALK

You know the rut of get up, take a shower, make coffee, and go to work. Instead, go for a morning walk.

A little change of scenery can make a big difference. You don't need to walk a thousand MILES. Two to three thousand steps makes a difference (get a Fitbit or an Apple watch!), and of course, it doesn't hurt if you're by the beach, or water.

HERE'S THE SECRET:

Walk breeds thoughts. Your mind is free to think and new ideas will appear. Text them to yourself. Some days I used to walk all the way over the Brooklyn Bridge. I walked off the stress, got a few ideas, and I burned a few calories. A walk can make a major difference.

A morning rut means you're probably in a daily rut. A sales rut. Walk it off and you'll get new ideas and new inspiration in a New York Minute.

DO THIS:

GET THE REST OF MY SLUMP-KICKING STRATEGIES.

Go to *27winningstrategies.com* and download my Ebook, *27 Winning Strategies That Will Take You From Sales Slump to Winning Streak.*

27winningstrategies.com

27
STRATEGIES
THAT WILL TAKE YOU
FROM SALES SLUMP TO
Winning
Streak
BY JENNIFER GLUCKOW

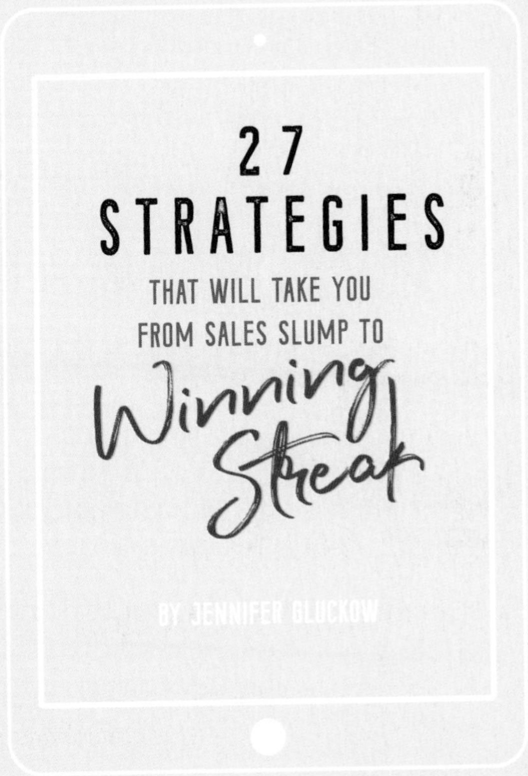

SALES IN A NY MINUTE
JENNIFER GLUCKOW

SERVICE MATTERS!

Outstanding, personal, and friendly customer service is underrated. And sometimes, it's lost as a priority. When you consider how automated and computerized the global marketplace has become, it's a tragedy for big business – but it's a HUGE opportunity for you. Providing personalized and memorable customer service is one of the few controllable variables in your business. You may not be able to control what caused the mistake or error, but you have 100% control over how you respond. And how you recover.

HERE'S THE SECRET:

Fast response, helpful information, and courteous demeanor give you the ability to fix a mistake beyond the customer's expectations. Great service will help you gain a competitive advantage and it'll earn you a great reputation by both word of mouth and word of mouse.

Oh, and by the way, it leads to genuine customer loyalty. Service matters and memorable service wins every time. The quality of yours will lead you to keep the customer, or lose the customer, in a New York Minute.

YOU MAY NOT BE ABLE
TO CONTROL WHAT
CAUSED THE MISTAKE OR
ERROR, BUT YOU HAVE
100% CONTROL OVER
HOW YOU RESPOND.
AND HOW YOU RECOVER.
SERVICE MATTERS AND
MEMORABLE SERVICE
WINS EVERY TIME.

JENNIFER GLUCKOW
@JENINANYMINUTE

NYC COFFEE HOUSE

SALES IN A NY MINUTE
JENNIFER GLUCKOW

BEING FRIENDLY MATTERS

Ever walk into a retail store where the salespeople were "too busy" texting, or chatting with colleagues, to offer help, or even just say hello? HELLO!? This happens all the time in New York City.

As a professional saleswoman, and eager retail customer, I approach the salesperson in the store and I let them know that I came to spend money, but since they're too busy to say hello, I'm going to the competition. The embarrassed salesperson, realizing that they've lost an opportunity for commission, looks somewhere between disappointed and shocked. But in New York, with all the other stores available, it's too late, they've lost their chance.

Ask yourself: How fast do you engage?

How responsive are you when a customer or prospect walks in, reaches out, emails or calls? That's what New York minutes are all about.

Pay attention to anything but your phone and your co-workers. If you want to increase your opportunities, be responsive, be friendly, be ready, and be engaging all the time. If you're immediately friendly, engaging, and responsive, you'll be earning more sales, and ringing your cash register, in a New York Minute.

TAKE ACTION:

Here's my friendly challenge: Practice engaging by talking to 5 strangers a day. You can chat up strangers anywhere - in grocery stores, at the movies, while commuting, in elevators (Yes! A major New York faux pas). My partner, Jeffrey, does this and he even takes it a step further by trying to make them laugh.

Check your responsiveness: On a scale of 1 to 5, rate yourself on your friendliness, your responsiveness and how engaging you are on a consistent everyday basis.

Ways to improve your responsiveness: Give every customer your cell phone number. Make a commitment to respond the same day to every inquiry, every customer request - it's okay to say you're working on their request - just don't leave them hanging without a response.

Do what you say you're going to do. If you say you will send the proposal by Tuesday at noon, send it by Tuesday at noon.

HOW RESPONSIVE ARE YOU WHEN A CUSTOMER OR PROSPECT WALKS IN, REACHES OUT, EMAILS OR CALLS?

JENNIFER GLUCKOW
@JENINANYMINUTE

LACK OF SERVICE, LACK OF CUSTOMERS

Lack of service, lack of friendliness, lack of apology for errors, and lack of service follow-through, leads to lack of sales...

AND EVENTUALLY LOSS OF CUSTOMER.

Not just the loss of one customer, but with social sharing, your poor service "secret" can lead to a social storm, and the loss of many customers – both current and potential.

READ THIS AND RELATE:

Ever try to buy something online and read the negative reviews about the seller or the product? Don't you go somewhere else to buy? Whether it's the post office or FedEx, whether it's Macy's or Bloomingdales, or whether it's McDonald's or Burger King, bad service by one business will lead to a gained customer by the other business in a New York Minute. How's your service?

SALES IN A NY MINUTE
JENNIFER GLUCKOW

MIXING SALAD WITH PATIENCE

Sweet Green is my favorite lunch place in New York City. But if you go during peak hours you could wait on line for 30 minutes - and I have and I'll continue to do so. In New York City, there are other salad places within a few blocks, but I choose to wait for my salad. Why do I wait? I wait for their quality, friendliness, and their consistency. They have proven to me time after time that they're well worth the wait and the money.

WOULD YOUR CUSTOMERS WAIT FOR YOU?

If you deliver quality with consistency and build good rapport, your customers will wait, and be loyal to you in a New York Minute.

TAKE ACTION:

Ask yourself, would you wait 30 minutes to meet with yourself? (For the record - don't keep your customer's waiting! Just ask yourself if a meeting with you is worth the wait.) Are you giving your customers enough value during your meeting to make it worth the wait? If not, work on improving your quality and consistency through the value you offer during every customer interaction. I promise it will improve loyalty in a New York Minute!

SALES IN A NY MINUTE
JENNIFER GLUCKOW

SALES FOOD
FOR THOUGHT

The other night I almost had the most amazing meal. The only problem was my food never came. Imagine going out to dinner, you're hungry, you're waiting and waiting and waiting for your food, and it just doesn't come. The waiter took no responsibility whatsoever. The manager came over and she was lasseiz-faire about it. She did comp a few of the meals, but at the end of the night, I still didn't receive my dinner.

Tonight my partner asked if I wanted to go to that same restaurant next week because the food was so good. You know what my response was? "What food? What was so good? I didn't eat!" They may have comped his meal, but they didn't fix the situation for me, making me not want to return. In bad service situations, our family friend used to say, "Take my picture, because you'll never see my face again!"

What do you do in a service situation? How do you handle it? How do you empower your people, your managers, to handle service situations and service recovery? Imagine if the waiter had come over and instead of shirking his responsibilities and making all kinds of excuses for why he didn't deliver my meal, he said, "I want to prove to you that we have some food in the kitchen. All you need to do is come back here and the next meal is on us!" I would have been back there tomorrow.

WHAT ARE YOU DOING TO MAKE YOUR CUSTOMERS SATISFIED WHEN SOMETHING'S GONE WRONG?

HERE'S WHAT TO DO:

Do something extra special - something that's going to make them say, "Yes! I want to go back. Yes! I want to do business with them again, and Yes! I want to post a review about it." In certain situations, you can't give away the whole thing - if something goes wrong with a car, you can't give them a new car, but you can give them an oil change or you can give them an amazing power wash.

MY CHALLENGE TO YOU:

There is always something you can do that will give extra value and wow your customer's expectations. Think past the situation to what may be the next interaction.

Create an amazing service recovery plan for your most common service issues and you'll be creating more loyal customers in a New York Minute.

IN BAD SERVICE SITUATIONS, OUR FAMILY FRIEND USED TO SAY, "TAKE MY PICTURE, BECAUSE YOU'LL NEVER SEE MY FACE AGAIN!"

JENNIFER GLUCKOW
@JENINANYMINUTE

CUSTOMER CELEBRATION

It's your customer's anniversary – not their wedding anniversary, their anniversary working with you! Do you show your customers appreciation? American Express, Mercedes Benz, and other businesses do – and guess what? They're on to something.

Everyone likes to feel appreciated – why not make your customers feel appreciated? Let them know that you value their business. Show your customers that you're proud and that you appreciate that they chose you. Celebrate and appreciate their loyalty. Make them know you are happy to serve them. How? Bring them together for an educational meeting, or take them to dinner, or host a customer appreciation night where your clients can network with each other.

DO THIS:

Showing even the smallest bit of appreciation will go a long way and will lead to even more business in a New York Minute.

SALES IN A NY MINUTE
JENNIFER GLUCKOW

CUSTOMER SERVICE VS. CUSTOMER HELP

Many people confuse customer service with a much more powerful phrase: **Customer Help**. Service is about being polite and being friendly. Help is about meeting or exceeding the customer's needs or desires.

CUSTOMER SERVICE IS EXPECTED.
CUSTOMER HELP IS NOTICED AND REMEMBERED.

Help, when someone goes above and beyond to make the client happy, is not only noticed and remembered, it's shared – it's shared in-person, it's shared on Facebook, it's shared on LinkedIn, on Twitter, it's shared globally.

TRY THIS COMBO:

When you combine great customer service and genuine customer help, you'll have loyal customers for a long, long time at high, high profit in a New York Minute.

SALES IN A NY MINUTE
JENNIFER GLUCKOW

DO THEY LIKE YOU?

If they do, they may be willing to pay you. Jeffrey Gitomer has a saying, "If they like you, and they believe you, and they have confidence in you, and they trust you, then they MAY buy from you."

NOTICE IT ALL STARTS WITH LIKE.

If you're not likeable, now's a real good time to get out of sales. Think about the people who like you – notice a trend? My friends and some of my favorite people are genuine, they're trustworthy, confident, they're happy, positive, giving people. Oh yeah, and they're *likeable*.

TAKE ACTION:

HOW LIKEABLE ARE YOU? DO YOUR CUSTOMERS LIKE YOU? LIKEABLE AND ITS SISTER, FRIENDLY, IS A STATE OF MIND, NOT JUST A PERSONALITY TRAIT.

What state are you in? Your friendliness and likeability will lead to more sales in like a New York Minute.

"

MEET PEOPLE
that matter
AND BE A
VALUE
PROVIDER

JENNIFER GLUCKOW
@JENINANYMINUTE

SALES IN A NY MINUTE
JENNIFER GLUCKOW

HOW DO YOUR RELATIONSHIPS RELATE TO YOU?

How's your relationship with your best customer? Would they WANT to go to dinner with you? Will it last decades because it's built on a solid foundation of common ground and rapport? Service? Value?

Want more sales and more referrals? **Here's a hint:** It's all about the depth and quality of your relationships.

TAKE ACTION:

Think about your best customer, eh, think about your top five customers. What do you have in common with each of them?

Think about your relationship with them. On a scale of 1, being not-so-friendly and 10, being uber-friendly, how is it?

Now, think about what you need to do to replicate those relationships with 10 more customers. What questions do you need to ask? What value do you need to provide? What quality relationship-building time do you need to spend?

The more you can improve your customer relationships, the more sales and referrals you will make in a New York Minute.

SALES IN A NY MINUTE
JENNIFER GLUCKOW

VIDEO-BASED SELLING IS THE NEW VALUE-BASED SELLING

Imagine this: You haven't spoken to your friend or a family member in a while and instead of getting a plain text message or email from them, you get a video message that's customized and personalized for you. It's emotional and real, and you love it!

Now imagine this: You get a video message from a vendor - your plumber, your HVAC company, any vendor, thanking you with appreciation for doing business with them. WOW!

Both of those are an unexpected WOW! Think about the emotion you might feel after receiving a personalized video.

Why aren't you doing this? Think of the power and surprise you can create. You can create that same emotional connection you felt from others with your clients and prospects.

What are you doing to create that emotional connection with your customers and prospects? What are you doing to keep in touch with your customers? Why are you not using your smartphone to make videos? It only takes a minute to create an emotional connection. Make one now!

DO THIS:

After you meet a prospect, send them a video message through text or email letting them know how great it was to meet with them and how you hope to do business with them. Set time aside on your calendar to send video messages to your current customers each month. SHOW THAT YOU CARE, don't just tell them you care.

YOUR CUSTOMERS AND PROSPECTS WANT TO GET TO KNOW YOU, NOT YOUR HIDDEN FACE BEHIND A SCREEN OR A TEXT-BASED MESSAGE.

And, they will feel special and more connected when you take an extra minute to create a video. It takes just that - a New York Minute.

Video messages will:

- Accelerate the trust factor.
- Accelerate the relational factor.
- Accelerate the emotional connection.
- Reaffirm their purchase after the sale.
- Create the WOW!

NOTE ON VIDEO MESSAGES:

Don't ever send a, "Hey, just sending you a video message to check in. Look at my view!" That message is all about you. Send a *value* video message, or a personal video message. Something they will get and immediately want to share with others.

VALUE-BASED
SELLING
BEGINS WITH
VIDEO-BASED
SELLING
AND WOW-ING
your customers
IN A NEW YORK MINUTE.

JENNIFER GLUCKOW
@JENINANYMINUTE

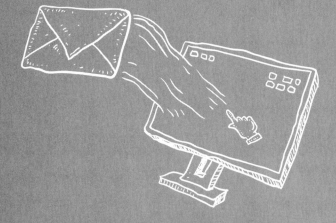

SALES IN A NY MINUTE

JENNIFER GLUCKOW

THE BEST WAY
TO GET REFERRALS

Everyone wants referrals, but most people make the mistake of asking for them. Bad.

The *best* way to get referrals is to become known as the person who GIVES referrals. Give to get, not ask to get. Just because you give a referral to someone, doesn't mean they will return the favor, but someone will give you a referral. It's way more than, "What comes around, goes around." It's "What you give around, comes back around." The key is giving without expectation.

Think of your clients, networking partners, vendors, people you have long-term relationships with and people you trust, and offer to introduce them to other people within your network. It's hard to do - that's why so few do it.

HERE'S WHAT TO DO:

Scroll through your list of contacts, especially people you haven't connected with in a while, and think about who you can make introductions for. Making an introduction that could lead to a sale is one of the greatest sources of value you can provide. The referral has to go both ways - the more referrals you give, the more you'll get in a New York Minute.

" WHAT YOU GIVE AROUND,

comes back around. "

JENNIFER GLUCKOW
@JENINANYMINUTE

SALES IN A NY MINUTE
JENNIFER GLUCKOW

HOW TO INTRODUCE
A REFERRAL

Don't just make an introduction, sell it! Explain why you believe they need to meet. Your explanation begins with belief - belief that each party will benefit from meeting the other, and that the introduction you're making is valuable.

KEEP IN MIND THAT THE REFERRAL IS A REFLECTION OF YOU AND THE RELATIONSHIPS OF TRUST THAT YOU HAVE BUILT. REFERRALS ARE RISKS. TAKE THE SAFE, SURE ONES.

The best way to make an introduction is to set a three-way introduction call. If you can't make the intro meeting, follow up and follow through. Find out if they were able to connect. Did it work out? Did it lead to a sale? Go one step beyond what most people do and learn what works and doesn't work for the people in your network. Hey, you'd want them to do the same for you! Plus, the people you refer will see your value and your dedication.

HERE'S THE SECRET:

Making valuable referrals is a triple win. Your referral connections benefit and you'll become known as a person of value (and one who others want to help!) in a New York Minute.

FOLLOWING UP
WITH A REFERRAL

SALES GOLD! You just got a referral! (Insert confetti celebration!)

Word-of-mouth referrals often result in quicker sales, *if* you follow the right path. It's by no means a "sure thing," *but* it is a valuable thing and a profitable thing because sales through referrals are more likely to buy and are less likely to hammer price.

It starts with a modicum of trust based on the person referring.

Think about this: Everyone has that friend who talks about stuff they purchased and raves so much that it makes you want to buy! When a connection or a referral comes through someone the prospect trusts, they're saying, "I bought from this guy or gal, and they're *great!*" That instills instant confidence before you even meet!

SPECIAL NOTE:

When someone gives you a referral, unless they specifically make an introduction, it's a lead, and NOT a referral. For example, if you're told, "Hey call Joe, he needs something," that's a lead. An actual introduction is a referral. Referrals will lead to more profit and more commission in a New York Minute.

REPUTATION, REPEAT CUSTOMER, AND REFERRAL

In today's social society, you can no longer "get away" with anything – poor quality, high pricing, and poor service are no longer tolerated and are posted online for all to see. Your "reputation truth" is exposed in a New York Minute on anyone's smartphone.

AND IN TODAY'S SOCIAL WORLD, THE REPEAT CUSTOMER, THE RECOMMENDED CUSTOMER, AND THE REFERRED CUSTOMER ARE THE HEART OF BUSINESS SUCCESS.

Here are the secrets to reputation, repeat customer, recommended customer, and referral:

- **Transfer your genuine passion and belief.** Keyword - genuine. If you love and believe in your products and services, you should have an easy time transferring your passion. Turn your customers into believers, and they too should have an easy time transferring their passion and making referrals.

- **Concentrate on helping, not making commissions.** Your help will earn their trust. Trust leads to long-term relationships. Trust leads to repeat business. Trust leads to referrals. Commissions will follow automatically.

- **Don't sell someone something they don't need**, or something that won't help them or they won't benefit from. In other words, only sell something that you believe helps the other guy.

HERE'S THE REALITY:

If they get home and realize they really didn't want it, need it or won't benefit from it, you will be blamed in seconds and your business reputation will be at risk.

Serve and help, not sell, and you'll be on your way to repeat and referral customers in a New York Minute.

JENNIFER GLUCKOW
@JENINANYMINUTE

"THEIR TRUST LEADS TO YOUR LONG-TEAM RELATIONSHIPS. TRUST LEADS TO REPEAT BUSINESS. TRUST LEADS TO REFERRALS."

EARN TESTIMONIALS

Make a plan to insure and ensure customer happiness and confidence.

Make an appointment to follow up with the customer to make sure they got what they purchased, and they're happy with their delivery plan or implementation process. Solidify your relationship so that you can earn a testimonial in the near future.

A lot of salespeople (not you, of course) think that when the sale is over, it's time to let the inside team handle it, so that they can move on to the next sale. And, of course, you should always be hustlin'...But, STOP! PAUSE. Customer gold lies ahead...

HERE'S THE LESSON:

When the sale is over, and you've done a great job, that's a great time to capitalize on your work, offer more help, take care of any and all issues, and earn a testimonial. Your customer will want to brag about how you helped them and how you can help others.

Earn that testimonial, and you'll be making your next sale in a New York Minute.

OUTSTANDING, PERSONAL,
AND FRIENDLY CUSTOMER SERVICE
IS UNDERRATED.

And sometimes, it's lost as a priority.

JENNIFER GLUCKOW
@JENINANYMINUTE

SALES IN A NY MINUTE
JENNIFER GLUCKOW

6WS OF TESTIMONIALS
- AND ONE AHA!

WHO. Get testimonials from your best customers. Your most raving fans. Your biggest advocates. Make sure they are presentable and relatable on camera.

WHAT. Ask them to talk about working with you, why they decided to work with you, or what held them back from switching to you (if something did). Make sure they are relaxed and ask them in question and conversational form so that they appear natural on camera. You can always edit if you need to!

WHERE. Film them in their office, over lunch, at a coffee shop, at your place of work, on a zoom.us meeting, anywhere. Just make sure the sound quality and picture quality rock.

WHEN. The best time to get a testimonial is after you've done the work and your customer has benefited from the work. Not before delivery and not before they are seeing results from working with you.

WHY. The second you show a customer testimonial, you become more believable and more trustworthy.

HOW. Ask for it like this: Would you mind if...Would it be okay if... But ask for it gently. And, a note on filming, you can use your iPhone - it doesn't have to be done by the pros.

AHA! Testimonials are also known as, "voice of customer." They are the proof that will convince customers and prospects when you are not able.

MAKE IT HAPPEN...

"

USE THE VOICE
OF OTHERS
TO PROVE
YOU DESERVE THE SALE
IN A NEW YORK MINUTE

JENNIFER GLUCKOW
@JENINANYMINUTE

TRANSFORM YOUR
WORK LIFE AND REAL LIFE.

HERE'S TO YOUR LIFE!

JENNIFER GLUCKOW
@JENINANYMINUTE

FROM WORK LIFE TO REAL LIFE AND BACK

Everybody needs a job or a business to support their family or their lifestyle, but everybody also has a life beyond the business, beyond the workday. And those two things, work and life, have to have some kind of harmony or balance or both.

I don't have a lot of balance, but I do have a lot of work and a lot of life. I afford myself time to run a business, be a speaker, be an author, and travel to cool places to do fun and inspiring things.

What's your life like? Are you working for the weekend or are you working for legacy? Are you working to have a party? Or are you working to make a community difference?

Because of technology, the world is closer, more transparent, more informed, and easier to traverse. How are you taking advantage of your life opportunities? And your lifelong relationships?

This section will provide you with insight about things you can do in your life and with your life that you may never have thought of: educational things, inspirational things, musical things, magical things, and just plain fun things.

SALES IN A NY MINUTE
JENNIFER GLUCKOW

YOUR MORNING ROUTINE: IS IT SALES WHEATIES OR IS IT WHAT'S ON YOUR PHONE?

Wake up and smell the lost opportunity.

What's the first thing you do when you get out of bed? Check your phone? Let me guess, you need to check the news? Or social media? Or email?

Morning PP: After *pee*, your next move should be *produce*.

ASK YOURSELF:

How is that productive to the start of your day? Most people (not you, right?) wake up and check their phones. It's become habit. You wake up and want to know what everyone else did overnight. Instead of being so concerned with what others are doing, make something happen for yourself.

"But Jen, in the morning I only check social media for 15 minutes and 15 minutes isn't a big deal." 15 minutes?! 15 minutes a day is 105 minutes a week, otherwise known as 91 hours a year, or 3.8 days a year - Eeek! Imagine what you could do with 4 extra days a year?

HERE'S THE REALITY:

Pictures on social media will be there later, your messages will be waiting for you, and you're not going to affect the news whether you check it or not. Stop worrying or investing in other people's lives. Invest in yourself first.

It's not just about waking up and eating your sales Wheaties. It's about waking up and fueling your mind, fueling your body, and giving your mind and body the kick-start it needs. It's about feeding your morning a box of champions.

MAKE IT COUNT:

Wake up and be intentional and productive with your morning actions every morning and you'll be gaining 4 days of time in almost a New York Minute.

Hint - need a better way to start your morning? Keep reading the next minute…

"STOP INVESTING IN
other people's lives or drama.
INVEST IN YOUR OWN LIFE FIRST."

JENNIFER GLUCKOW
@JENINANYMINUTE

SALES IN A NY MINUTE
JENNIFER GLUCKOW

MORNING SALES FUEL.
LIFE FUEL. YOUR MORNING ROUTINE.

Most people don't have a solid morning routine. Luckily, you're not like most people.

Successful people *do* have a morning routine! A morning ritual. A daily morning success plan.

WAKE UP CALL:

Jeffrey Gitomer and I interviewed Hal Elrod, Author of *The Miracle Morning* on our podcast, *Sell or Die*. You can listen to the episode by going to: *salesinanyminutebook.com/sellordie*. I used to wake up and immediately check Instagram, insta-eeek! Plus, snooze was a major part of my daily routine. Now it's up, out, and rock the day.

I accomplish more before 6AM than many people accomplish in a day. What do you accomplish before 6AM?

The foundation of my personal morning routine comes from *The Miracle Morning*. Hal invented the SAVERS method - it stands for Silence (prayer or meditation), Affirmations, Visualization, Exercise, Reading and Scribing (writing).

You can download my morning hacks to achieve amazing morning success here: *salesinanyminutebook.com/savers*. End your morning routine with your morning playlist and you'll be ready to rock 'n roll.

Just like with building a home or your career, the foundation is most important. Your foundation, your daily foundation, is critical to your creativity, problem-solving ability and your success.

Don't give me excuses that you gotta get your kids off to school, or walk the dogs, or some other excuse. Wake up an hour earlier than you're waking up now and crush it.

YOUR ACTION:

You need to create a ritual that gets you so pumped to take action. A ritual that transforms you and helps you become more successful day-by-day.

If your day starts right, it's more than likely to end right - even if something goes wrong mid-day. I have bad minutes, eh, they're not even minutes, they're New York Minutes.

My morning routine has changed my life. It sounds serious, 'cause it is. What's your morning routine? Is it helping you or hurting you?

What's in your morning gas tank?
If it's only coffee, you need more than a one hour pick-me-up.

When you create a transformative morning routine and make it a habit, you'll be having AMAZING days every day in a New York Minute.

IF YOU DON'T SWEAT, YOU DON'T GET.

Wake up and work out. Is that you?

Sounds simple. Some days it's easier than others. When you're tired and want to sleep in, and you push yourself to wake up and sweat a little, your sense of accomplishment is that much more rewarding. Especially if you're finished working out before most people are even awake!

Your morning routine directly affects what you'll accomplish during the day.

DO THIS:

After a good sweat, immediately write your positive thoughts and ideas, and focus on the detail of tasks you must accomplish for the day.

When you sweat to get, you'll be dripping achievement. If you're willing to SWEAT, I promise you'll GET, more sales in a New York Minute.

PUT YOURSELF
FIRST

WAKE UP AND READ,
WRITE, AND WORKOUT.
only then can you be your
BEST SELF FOR OTHERS.

JENNIFER GLUCKOW
@JENINANYMINUTE

CAROLE KING... MUSICIAN, LYRICIST, OR SALESWOMAN? YES!

Well besides the fact that she's one of the most successful songwriters of the 20th century and has sold more than 75 million records, CDs and iTunes downloads worldwide (now that's a lot of sales!), her lyrics in the Broadway smash hit "Beautiful" set the tone for how you need to start each day.

She wrote,

"YOU'VE GOT TO GET UP EVERY MORNING,
WITH A SMILE ON YOUR FACE,
AND SHOW THE WORLD ALL THE LOVE IN YOUR HEART,
THEN PEOPLE GONNA TREAT YOU BETTER,
YOU'RE GONNA FIND, YES YOU WILL,
THAT YOU'RE BEAUTIFUL, AS YOU FEEL."

How you feel on the inside is how you'll be treated on the outside. Wake up with a smile on your face, or not, and you'll find your interactions with people are positive, or not. You decide. Your self-love, self-confidence and optimism will be contagious in a New York Minute.

DO THIS:

For the next 30 days, in the morning, look in the mirror and smile. Tell yourself you're going to have a great, successful, happy day. You may want to play "Beautiful" in the background as you look in the mirror. It's my morning anthem. When you see how well this works, and the positivity it brings to your day, you'll want to keep going past 30 days.

"IF YOU DON'T GO FORWARD, YOU'RE GONNA GO BACK HEY, YOU BETTER GET A PLAN OF ATTACK 'CAUSE THAT'S THE ONLY WAY THAT YOU'RE GONNA KEEP TRACK OF YOUR LEGACY."

CAROLE KING

SALES IN A NY MINUTE
JENNIFER GLUCKOW

STUCK IN A HOLE?

A hole is another word for problem, issue, tough situation or worse. The severity of the hole is often measured by its depth - some people are in over their ankles - and some are in over their heads.

Here are a few holes to consider. As I mention them to you, think how they apply:

- Sales holes - can't close a big deal - can't make quota.
- Financial holes - behind on payments - big credit card debt.
- Relationship holes - arguing with spouse - relationship with customers.
- Career holes - can't advance - can't get a raise - hate your job.
- Family holes - family members in trouble.
- Or maybe you've just stepped in a hole and twisted your ankle. A health issue.

GRAB YOUR SHOVEL AND PUT ON YOUR WORK BOOTS. YOU ARE THE ONLY ONE WHO CAN DIG YOURSELF INTO OR OUT OF A HOLE.

It all begins with YOU - your attitude, your self-belief, your hustle and your desire and dedication to hard work.

HERE ARE A FEW INSIGHTS TO HELP GET BACK TO LEVEL GROUND:

- Surround yourself with positive and supportive people.
- Stay positive. Stay strong.
- Material things are just that - material.
- Rally behind something you're passionate about.
- Connect and reconnect with your network.
- Find your purpose and commit it to writing.

You can't change others, but you can be responsible for yourself and your actions.

UNDERSTAND AND DISSECT FAILURES TO DISCOVER OPPORTUNITIES. BUY A SHOVEL. START DIGGING. AND YOU'LL FIND YOUR BURIED TREASURE WITHIN A NEW YORK MINUTE.

IT ALL BEGINS WITH YOU-YOUR ATTITUDE. YOUR SELF-BELIEF. YOUR HUSTLE. YOUR DESIRE. AND DEDICATION TO HARD WORK.

JENNIFER GLUCKOW
@JENINANYMINUTE

YOU DETERMINE YOUR PATH WITH YOUR PASSION AND YOUR PURPOSE

What road are you on? Are you creating your own yellow brick road or blindly walking down the road without any sort of GPS?

You can create or change your path with your passion and your purpose. And then use your power as your guide. Passion, purpose, path, power - the 4 P's that lead to the ultimate "P" - profit.

By "profit," don't just think of the true definition of the word - a financial gain. Your profit can be any gain or success you are aiming for - a strengthened relationship, a career win, weight loss, weight gain and of course, a financial gain, You name it - it's your road, your roadmap, and your success.

GRAB YOUR IMPLE-MENTOR
Now here's how you make this real for yourself...

Ask yourself:
What's your path? Is it the one you want? Or is it time for a new direction?
What's your passion? What's your purpose? What's your power?

Document and define your P's in writing. Review them. Revise them.
Then go buy a rake and use it on your profits, in a New York Minute.

AND REMEMBER...

66

IT'S PROGRESS, NOT PERFECTION.
IT'S PRACTICE
THAT TAKES
PATIENCE.
IT'S PLANNED PREPARATION AND
PRESENCE THAT CREATE
POWER, PERFORMANCE,
AND PROFIT

JENNIFER GLUCKOW
@JENINANYMINUTE

A GIVER, A TAKER, AND AN EQUALIZER ALL WALK INTO A BAR.

There are three types of people:

Givers: people who give without expectation. No tit-for-tat. Just give wholeheartedly every time. It's not just about giving a donation or volunteering time, it's about making an introduction, helping someone grow their business by giving them advice or knowledge, or mentoring someone. The key is no strings attached.

Takers: people whose natural instinct is to take first and maybe do something in return.

Equalizers: People who give, but expect to get an equal amount back in return. You know those people who say, "I gave you this, so I expected you to do that..."

Which one are you?

Personal Story: I was invited to visit a networking group, a somewhat exclusive group of people, who were at the top of their game and successful. This was a group of people I knew I could learn from, and who could learn from me.

I was told to show up with a prepared script of what I did and who I was looking to meet. That felt uncomfortable - check out the group, and see what I could GET? No.

I asked if instead, I could GIVE a 20-minute LinkedIn lesson to show everyone how they could use LinkedIn to get more business.

Not only were they excited by the prospect of my talk, but after my talk and before I even left the meeting, they asked if I would join.

MY ABILITY AND DESIRE TO GIVE MADE ALL THE DIFFERENCE. I DIDN'T GIVE TO GET. I GAVE BECAUSE I WANTED TO ESTABLISH A FOUNDATION OF TRUST AND REAL RELATIONSHIP.

I GAVE BECAUSE I WANTED TO SET THE FOUNDATION OF MY DESIRE TO "GIVE NOT GET."

REALITY: your giving doesn't have to start with a talk, it can start with coffee and maybe offer a sales lead or possible connection for the other person. Or it could start the other way around – meet someone you believe you could help and offer to connect over a coffee to talk about it. The key is to have no expectations in return.

DO THIS:

Give without expectation. Check yourself when you give to make sure you are not measuring or expecting something in return. Give daily and freely and you'll be getting more than you can imagine in a New York Minute.

"DO YOU REALLY
give without expectation?
OR DO YOU REMEMBER
WHAT YOU GAVE AND
EXPECT SOMETHING BECAUSE
'THEY OWE YOU ONE'?"

JENNIFER GLUCKOW
@JENINANYMINUTE

WHAT INSPIRES YOU?

Paris and New York set the standard for other cities.

What are your standard setters?
List three things that inspire you.
List three places that inspire you.
List three people that inspire you.
Think about what inspires you and...think about why.

The "what" will excite you and inspire you. The "why" will give you the insight and the wisdom. Understanding your what and your why will help you set the standard for your sales and your life. It may not be Paris for you – set your standards by your own inspirations. It may be the food in Jersey City or the museum in St. Louis – whatever it is, your inspirational standards set the stage for your inspirational messaging. And that will lead to an inspired life in a New York Minute.

GRAB YOUR IMPLE-MENTOR
Dig into your inspiration.

BIG PICTURE, NARROW FOCUS

How many things are you focused on right now? Tasks. Numbers. Quota. Sales Plan. Follow-up. Sales. Customers. Businesses. Projects, even your personal projects.

IF YOU WANT TO BECOME REALLY GOOD AT ONE THING,
YOU NEED TO FOCUS ON THAT ONE THING.

While everyone thinks they're the best multitaskers on the planet, the truth is, they're not, and the more you delegate tasks and narrow your focus, the more successful you will become.

I challenge you to funnel your attention to one area for the next 90 days. You don't need to be good at everything. You need to be great at *some* thing - *one* thing. You need to be really good at delegating little things and focusing on one thing. You need to become the expert in your field.

For the next 2-3 months, put your greatness eggs in one basket, and as it works, continue to keep them there. With sheer focus and dedication, you'll be on your way to massive success in a New York Minute.

TAKE ACTION:

ASK YOURSELF:

What's the one thing you want to accomplish or excel at in the next 12 months? Something you want to achieve expert status in. What priorities do you need to drop in order to focus on your goal?

KEEP YOUR EYE ON THE BALL YOUR FINGER ON THE PULSE...

YOUR HEAD IN THE GAME AND YOUR ASS IN GEAR.

My tennis coach trains winners. He was training a young kid who kept hitting the ball into the net. He told the kid, "Talk to the ball as you hit it. Look at it, focus on it, and tell it you're gonna give it a great ride over the net." The key is self-talk and focus.

Wow, what a concept! With that one statement, the child is instilling self-belief that he WILL hit it over the net, and by talking to the ball, he's a hundred percent focused on looking at the ball as he is hitting it. He's training his mind to place his attention on one thing at a time.

Is your eye focused on the sale? How often do you apply dedicated moments of focus? How often do you have quality self-focus or self-talk moments throughout the day? How often do you just focus on your prospect or the task you need to complete to achieve your goal?

It's no surprise that my coach's method works. That kid got the next 10 balls over the net and into the court. That newfound confidence allowed him to strengthen the stroke and not only hit balls over the net but hit winning shots.

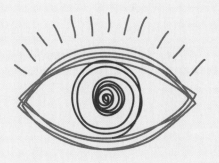

VISUALIZE YOURSELF WINNING.
TELL YOURSELF YOU'RE A WINNER, AND YOU WILL WIN.

Create direct focus on your intention to win, and you'll be on your way to becoming a superstar in a New York Minute.

JENNIFER GLUCKOW
@JENINANYMINUTE

LIFE · MINDSET

SALES IN A NY MINUTE
JENNIFER GLUCKOW

GOT MENTOR?

List your advisors. List your coaches. List the people you trust.

Now list your mentors. The people you trust to give you advice because they want to help you grow and succeed without a selfish reason and without measurement.

Look at your mentor list.
The quality of the list is commensurate to your success.

You need a mentor (or two) - whether you are new to sales or a sales-know-it all.

HERE'S WHY:

A mentor will give you real-world advice and encouragement when you need it the most. And the right mentor will have a network, and a rolodex, that they are willing to open to you when needed.

If you get the right mentor or mentors, they will become an integral part of your success. In fact, they will feel so invested in your success that they too will be celebrating your success when you find it.

Mentors, they do your sales, your success, and your life good, in a New York Minute.

SALES IN A NY MINUTE
JENNIFER GLUCKOW

NOT ALL MENTORS ARE CREATED EQUAL

Here are the 8 characteristics you need to look for in a mentor:

- **Success:** Their past history of success that relates to you.
- **KLTB Factor:** They must know, like, trust, and believe in you. And you must know, like, trust and believe that they can help you.
- **Experience:** Been there, done that is a good thing. They can help you avoid mistakes.
- **Direct communication:** They tell it like it is. And you adopt it.
- **Open:** Someone willing to discuss their failures, and lessons learned, not just their successes.
- **Responsive:** They're able to respond when you need them most, and you take notes when they do.
- **Generous:** Someone who will be generous with their time, advice, their knowledge and their contacts.
- **Cheerleader ability:** Forget the outfit. They need to be able to give you a pep (encouragement) talk and cheer you on during every game, major sale and major event.

IMPORTANT NOTE:

You have to have characteristics and charisma that your mentor finds attractive. Hard work, on the right track, high ethics. Truthful. When you find the right mentor, implement their advice, tell them what you did, thank them, and you'll be on the fast track to success in a New York Minute.

LIFE · MENTORS

JEN, HOW CAN I FIND A LIFELONG MENTOR?

When you're seeking a mentor, it's important to be compatible.

Mentors, "They're just like us," except more advanced and more successful in their career or your industry. They have "been there, done that, and can buy the T-shirt factory."

People ask me all the time, "Jen, How can I find a mentor?" The best mentors are **never** the result of you asking a successful stranger to be your mentor. Think about it, a mentor will give free help, shortcuts, ideas, and strategies, and use their time and potentially their contacts to make it happen **only if you earn their respect and trust**.

The secret to getting the perfect mentor to invest in you, is that mentors are **earned**, not asked for.

Think about who you already know, someone who has confidence in you and cares about your success, someone who is next-level or where you want to be in terms of success, career, relationships, life. Someone who is willing to give you advice and invest time to help you achieve the level of success you're hoping for.

If you don't know anyone, start by asking your network who they know that you could connect with. Or start networking.

THE KEY IS THE VALUE TO THEM

The best mentor relationships begin with a friendship and casual conversation. Don't ask someone to be your mentor. Let the relationship evolve over time. Let them offer to help you. It starts with you providing value to them. If you have to ask for mentorship, something's wrong - you haven't provided enough value.

Connect over coffee, get to know them, establish a friendship first. Give them a reason to want to help you by finding an emotional connection - a reason that would excite them to help you - a shared passion or a shared mission.

When you find the right mentor and they like you, your value, your moxie, and your shared vision, they'll gladly and freely mentor you to success in a New York Minute.

"THE SECRET TO GETTING THE PERFECT MENTOR TO INVEST IN YOU, IS THAT MENTORS ARE EARNED, WITH VALUE GIVEN AND ATTRACTION, NOT ASKED FOR."

JENNIFER GLUCKOW
@JENINANYMINUTE

SALES IN A NY MINUTE

JENNIFER GLUCKOW

WHO DO YOU CHOOSE
TO BE AROUND?

Think about the 5 people you hang around with the most:

- Are they inspirational?
- Are they successful?
- Are they mentally challenging you?
- Are they pushing you to do better?
- Or are they bringing you down, one negative comment at a time?

Think about this: Jim Rohn says, "You are the average of the five people you spend the most time with." Napoleon Hill, Author of *Think and Grow Rich* and arguably America's forefather of personal development, hung around the likes of Andrew Carnegie, Henry Ford, Harvey Firestone, and Thomas Edison. What a mastermind!

GRAB YOUR IMPLE-MENTOR

Find your career cheerleaders, find people who are successful and want to see you be successful, and surround yourself by them, and you'll be winning more in sales and in life, in a New York Minute.

IF YOU WANT
TO BE A
WINNER,
hang around people
WHO HAVE
⌐WON.⌐

JENNIFER GLUCKOW
@JENINANYMINUTE

SALES IN A NY MINUTE
JENNIFER GLUCKOW

HOW WELL DO YOU COMMUNICATE YOUR LOVE AND GRATITUDE?

Probably not well enough, and not often enough.

Think about the 5 most important people in your life. When was the last time you told them how much you love them or how grateful you are for them? Not a standard getting off the phone, "Love you, bye." Or an "I ♥ you" text, but rather taking a second, or a New York Minute, to tell someone how much they mean to you.

Anyone in your life you wish you could still call but they're no longer here?

Telling someone how much you care about them or how grateful you are for them, not only brightens their day, but also brightens your day. It's mood boosting, attitude boosting, and relationship boosting.

DO THIS:

Make a short list of the people you want to communicate gratitude to. Send a video message to one of your loved ones and tell them how grateful you are for them and why. Tell them you love them. Then do it for another, and another.

Try it today, and reap the reward for a lifetime.

Now think about your 5 best customers. You don't have to say, "I love you," but you should say, "I appreciate you."

COMMUNICATE YOUR LOVE AND APPRECIATION AND YOU'LL BE MAKING THE MOST IMPORTANT PEOPLE IN YOUR LIFE SMILE, AND YOU'LL BE SMILING YOURSELF, IN A NEW YORK MINUTE.

JANNIFER GLUCKOW
@JENINANYMINUTE

LIFE · GRATITUDE

SALES IN A NY MINUTE

JENNIFER GLUCKOW

30 DAY SUCCESS CHALLENGE

Before you give yourself a challenge, ask yourself these revealing questions:

- What are you doing right now that you wish you were not doing?
- What are you not doing that you wish you were?
- If you continue doing what you're doing right now every day, where will you be at the end of 6 months? At the end of a year? At the end of 5 years?
- Is that the potential outcome you're hoping for?

I have created a 30-day challenge to help of reinforce your achievement process.
Download: *salesinanyminute.com/goal-map*

Your challenge is to be honest with yourself. You may need to change your route, and correct your course because you can either drive to success or mediocrity, in a New York Minute.

YOUR PART

Here's your challenge...Over the next 30 days, beginning today (don't tell me you'll start tomorrow, or give me some lame-ass excuse for why you can't start today) do this:

☑ **Think about who you want to become.** Write about it and make it visible in a place where you can see it every day. Do this today.

☑ **Summarize who you want to become in 1 or 2 sentences.** This is your goal. Set a reminder on your phone to show up three times a day – morning (when you wake up), night time (before you go to bed) and sometime around lunch, to pop up and remind you of your goal. Seeing your goals numerous times a day will help keep you on path. Especially if you begin to steer off-route.

☑ **Within the first week, identify 3-5 accomplishments** you've made this year. They don't have to be accomplishments towards your goal. Just things you've done that you're proud of. Lost two pounds. Saved a hundred dollars. Made a sale. No matter how small, review your accomplishments and be proud of them.

☑ **Take note of your new accomplishments towards your goal.** Write them down in your workbook. Record them even if they are small accomplishments. On difficult days, review your list.

☑ **Use your new accomplishments to inspire next accomplishments.**

☑ **Direct your thoughts.** "We become what we think about" (Earl Nightingale). Stop thinking negative - why or how you're not where you want to be, and start thinking about what you have achieved and how you can achieve more.

☑ **Goal Secret**: The Daily Dose. Work on achieving your goal, and making small steps towards your goal every day. If you don't work at it every day, it will never get done.

Begin with your daily dose and you'll be achieving your goals in a New York Minute.

JENNIFER GLUCKOW

THE BEST WAY
TO SUCCEED IN LIFE

Many people think that the way to succeed in business is to look out for themselves. Rather than wonder, "What's in it for me?" you should be thinking about how to help others. If you focus on helping others succeed, you will build stronger relationships faster than you can imagine. Relationships where the other guy will wanna help YOU.

SO HERE'S HOW TO DO IT:

Listen and pay attention for clues to assist, make introductions that will help others grow their business - become known as the connector. Find articles, videos and content of value that will help the other guy grow, reduce costs, and profit more.

By helping others, you'll feel great and you'll be on your way to massive success in a New York Minute.

"IT IS LITERALLY TRUE THAT YOU CAN SUCCEED BEST AND QUICKEST BY HELPING OTHERS TO SUCCEED."
– NAPOLEON HILL

BECOME AN OVERNIGHT SALES SUCCESS IN A NY MINUTE, OR TWO, OR MORE

This book didn't get written overnight.

As I got close to the 212th page, I reflected on the fact that it's taken waaaaay more than a New York minute to complete this task.

Here's the deal: I created these strategies one by one, day by day, minute by minute. I created them with persistence, dedication, and hard work.

What are you putting your consistent effort into today that will lead to greater success tomorrow? You don't get good at sales (or anything!) overnight. You get good customer by customer, relationship by relationship, day by day, minute by minute, sale by sale. You get good with practice, study, persistence, dedication and hard work.

HERE'S MY CHALLENGE TO YOU:

Invest your time daily in something that will help you grow.
Day by day - like a vitamin - a sales vitamin. And within a year or two (or ten), you'll become an overnight success in a New York Minute.

THE BEST LIFELONG
INVESTMENT YOU CAN MAKE...

Is in yourself. How much time do you invest in your learning - Daily? Weekly? Monthly?

If you want to be the best, you need to take actions to become the best. Those actions include a daily commitment to learning.

This is not just about becoming the best salesperson - you have to read, study, and practice daily. If you want to be the best dad or mom, read books about parenting. If you want to be the best partner, read books about relationships. If you want to learn a language, an instrument, a new software, you've got to invest time into learning.

And it's no longer just about reading. My grandpa used to say, "JB (short for Jennifer Blake), everything you need to know can be learned from a book." It is ironic that he had a career printing books. Now everything you need to know can be learned online or from a podcast or a course or a book!

It's not just sell or die. It's learn or die. Without learning, you're not growing. Ever notice the word earn is in learn?
He also won an award for never missing a day of school in his life. But this is not about formal college or university education - this is about self-education, passion education, mastery education, best education.

Benjamin Franklin said,

"IF A MAN EMPTIES HIS PURSE INTO HIS HEAD NO
ONE CAN TAKE IT AWAY FROM HIM. AN INVESTMENT
IN KNOWLEDGE ALWAYS PAYS THE BEST INTEREST."

I say,

"WHEN YOU FILL YOUR BRAIN WITH KNOWLEDGE,
YOU FILL YOUR WALLET WITH GOLD
IN A NEW YORK MINUTE."

HERE'S WHAT TO DO:

Commit to the learning (and the implementation) it takes to become a
master salesperson.

Answer these questions:

- How many books or educational courses have you taken this year
  on becoming the best salesperson?
- How much time every day have you invested in the knowledge you
  need to become the best? (This book is a good start.)

Make a learning doubling plan - double your learning efforts. It may
mean skipping out on a dinner or cutting out aimless internet searches
for cat videos so that you can commit and schedule the time with
yourself. Commit to at least 30 minutes a day.

The key to learning is taking your knowledge and implementing what
you've learned.

LIFE · SUCCESS

INVEST YOUR TIME DAILY IN SOMETHING THAT WILL HELP YOU GROW.

AND WITHIN A YEAR OR TWO, YOU'LL
BECOME AN OVERNIGHT SUCCESS
IN A NEW YORK MINUTE.

THIS IS THE UNOFFICIAL END OF THE BOOK,
BUT NOT THE END OF THE GOLDEN OPPORTUNITY...

212

JENNIFER GLUCKOW
@JENINANYMINUTE

DOWNLOAD
YOUR IMPLE-MENTOR
NOW!

WORKBOOK

salesinanyminutebook.com/workbook

YOU'LL FIND ME HERE:

ALL MY INFORMATION
www.salesinanyminute.com

ALL MY SOCIAL...CONNECT WITH ME.
social.salesinanyminute.com

MY PERSONAL EMAIL
jen@salesinanyminute.com

THE BEST DAILY SALES AND
PERSONAL DEVELOPMENT PODCAST
ON THE PLANET

LISTEN. SUBSCRIBE. LEARN. SUCCEED.

sellordiepodcast.com

ALL OF THE RESOURCES
MENTIONED IN THIS BOOK
CAN BE FOUND AT

salesinanyminutebook.com

GET THE LATEST AND
GREATEST COURSES HERE:

courses.salesinanyminute.com

> " "

> STUDY HARD,
> **WORK HARDER,**
> **ENJOY LIFE HARDEST,**
> *in that order*

JENNIFER GLUCKOW
@JENINANYMINUTE

I'M GRATEFUL TO AND FOR...

I dedicate this book to Grandma Harriette who taught me to be my best and look my best. I am forever grateful for her unconditional love.

Thank you **JEFFREY**, my best friend, my partner (in life and business) and my forever mate. When the book deadline was approaching, *Jeffrey* took over my day-to-day responsibilities and sent me to the beach to write. His unconditional and unwavering support, love, and guidance, both in business and in life, is unprecedented. Whether I've needed help at 6 AM or midnight, Jeffrey has been by my side. Jeffrey's Yes! Attitude, creativity, humor, and quest to live life fully every day are inspiring and contagious. He is the true definition of a "giver" and I am forever grateful for his love and support.

To my **FAMILY**. *Mom* and *Dad*, thank you giving me first-class education, both in formal schooling and in business, for modeling work ethic and success, and for providing me with life-shaping travel opportunities. *Jordana*, thank you for your sassy sisterly love. And to my Cousin *Jessica*, *Aunt Aly* and *Grandma Glo*, thanks for your love and support.

To **JEFFREY'S FAMILY**. *Erika, Matt, Stacey, Rebecca, Mike, Gabrielle, Julia, Morgan, Claudia*, and *Isabel*, thank you for accepting me into your family. I am honored to be a part of it. And thank you for supporting me during the book process and the life process.

To my **WORK FAMILY**. I am surrounded by an amazing, smart, dedicated A+ team of real people. To *Erika* for her willingness and desire to help in work and life and for being a second mom to the dogs. To *Stacey* for making sure I am always where I need to be, for clearing my schedule so I could write, and being there to listen on the other end of the line. To *Lisa*, I am forever grateful for you working days, nights, and weekends to edit my book, for providing me with moral support, organization, laughs, thought-provoking ideas, positivity, dedication, and constant encouragement. And, thank you for being my genuine friend. To *Alex* for jumping in wherever needed and whenever needed without needing to be asked, always showing up with a happy and positive attitude, and with a desire and work ethic to create massive success. To *Ashley* for bringing my words to life with her creative design. To *Mike* for his speed, accuracy, and dedication at a time of genuine need. Your reliability, responsiveness, and genuine care are greatly appreciated. To *Doug* for his on-point and thought-provoking feedback and for challenging me to take my thoughts and ideas to the next level. You help me grow every time. To *Steve* for pushing my creativity and bringing a new level of comedy to my NY Minute videos. To *Nata* for your great coaching and patience. To *Brad* for reading and editing my book. And of course, to *Elizabeth* for taking care of me with her massive heart, and managing our space daily. She embodies the definition of "holding down the fort."

To my **PUBLISHER** and trusted book advisor, *Sound Wisdom and Dave Wildasin*. Thank you for believing in me as a first-time author, guiding and advising me along the way, and for helping me get my message out to the world.

To the **DOGS**. The first article I read about writing an acknowledgement page said, "Don't include your dogs." Oops! People say they're lucky dogs, but the truth is, I'm a lucky human. *Charlie* provides unconditional love and emotional support. Thank you for making me walk 14,000 steps a day, especially during my write-cation so you could find the perfect spot. And to *Zoe* for 212 kisses a day.

Thanks to *every prospect* who has turned me down, *every lead* who never returned my call, *every customer who didn't refer or renew*...thank you. Thank you for providing me with real-world lessons of acceptance and rejection that made me a better salesperson.

And to **YOU**, *my customer* for believing I can help, and your willingness to try these ideas and strategies. Please stay in touch on your journey. I would love to hear about your success.

Jen in a ny Minute

JENNIFER GLUCKOW

Jennifer Gluckow has northeastern smarts, New York City savvy, and southern charm – a rare combination that has her positioned as the next big thing in sales. Okay, she's not ALL New York. She's traveled the world, educated in the Midwest, and spoken to audiences from coast to coast.

She grew up in a successful family book manufacturing business run by her parents. Their dinner table conversations were an MBA real-world business education years before Jennifer graduated from the Olin School of Business at Washington University in St. Louis.

Jennifer rapidly rose through the ranks of a leading Fortune 500 company as a superstar Salesperson, National Sales Manager, and second in command of Sales. At 29, Jennifer became Chief Operating Officer of a test preparation and admissions counseling company.

In 2013 Jennifer found her calling – speaking to sales teams and business owners on how to increase their sales and make more profit. She founded Sales in a New York Minute and shares her passion and strategies for success with salespeople and businesses worldwide.

Her body of work includes *Jen's Top Ten for Sales Zen*, *57 Varieties of the Best Networking Opportunities and What To Do When You Get There*, *27 Winning Strategies that will take you from Sales Slump to Winning Streak* and hundreds of articles on sales and personal development.

Jennifer's a speaker, trainer, writer, blogger, Facebooker, Instagrammer, Tweeter, YouTuber and Podcaster. She is online and on the money. Her trademarked advice YouTube channel, Sales in a New York Minute, features short sales and life tips. Her podcast *Sell or Die*, with co-host Jeffrey Gitomer, gets over 100,000 downloads a month.

Drive, persistence, and winning through a desire to serve, have made Jennifer Gluckow an example of how to "make it" in New York, and her mission is to teach you how to make it anywhere.

Jen in a NY Minute

www.salesinanyminute.com
jen@salesinanyminute.com
(212) 951-1153

THE BEST

success advice

I CAN

GIVE ANY

SALESPERSON

IS:

LOVE WHAT YOU DO!

Jen in a NY Minute